Obstacles in your Way

Body Soul Flesh Heart
Spirit Mind Emotions Will

Give it to God Today

Sonya C. Greene- Pough

authorHOUSE

AuthorHouse™
1663 Liberty Drive
Bloomington, IN 47403
www.authorhouse.com
Phone: 833-262-8899

Published by AuthorHouse   10/21/2021

ISBN: 978-1-6655-3733-9 (sc)
ISBN: 978-1-6655-3732-2 (e)

CONTENTS

SALVATION

Romans 1:16 *For I am not ashamed of the* **Good News of Christ**, *because it is* **the power of God for salvation for everyone who believes.** _{WEB}

John 3:16-18 **For God so loved the world that He gave His one and only Son, that whoever believes in Him shall not perish but have eternal life.** *For God did not send His Son into the world to condemn the world, but* **to save the world through Him.** *Whoever believes in Him is not condemned, but whoever does not believe stands condemned already because they have not believed in the name of God's one and only Son.* _{WEB}

As many as who receive the Son Jesus, are the children of God. John 1:12 *But as many as received Him, to them He gave the right to become God's children, to those who believe in His name.* _{WEB}

For forgiveness of our sins, we must repent and be baptized in Jesus the Christ name. Acts 2:38 *Peter said to them,* **"Repent, and be baptized, every one of you, in the name of Jesus Christ for the forgiveness of sins,** *and you will receive the gift of the Holy Spirit.* _{WEB}

This is a gift of God, by His grace we are saved through our faith in Him. Ephesians 2:8 **for by grace you have been saved through faith,** *and that not of yourselves; it is the gift of God.* _{WEB}

Who needs salvation? We all need salvation according to Romans 3:23 *for all have sinned, and fall short of the glory of God.* _{WEB}

Why do we need salvation? We all need Salvation according to Romans 6:23 *For the wages of sin is death, but the free gift of God is eternal life in Christ Jesus our Lord.* _{WEB}

When was salvation provided for us? Romans 5:8 *But God commends His own love toward us, in that while we were yet sinners, Christ died for us.* _{WEB}

How do we receive salvation? Romans 10:9-10 *that if you will confess with your mouth that Jesus is Lord, and believe in your heart that God raised Him from the dead, you will be saved. For with the heart, one believes unto righteousness; and with the mouth confession is made unto salvation.* _{WEB}

JESUS IS THE ONLY NAME IN WHICH WE CAN BE SAVED. Acts 4:12 *There is salvation in none other, for neither is there any other name under heaven, that is given among men, in which we must be saved!* _{WEB}

How can you hear without a preacher? According to Colossians 1:25 a minister from God is to make the Word of God fully known. How can one preach except they be sent by God? Some were sent by God and some just went on their own. Others were sent by the enemy as angels of light to deceive us; they are called wolves in sheep's clothing.

We must lift the name above every other name. That name we are to lift is Jesus the Christ/Yeshua Ha Mashiach. If Christ be lifted, He will draw all of humankind unto Him. His name is the only name by which humankind can be saved.

You must be born again of the water and of the Spirit. The only way to be born of both the water and the Spirit is through Jesus. You must be baptized in His name for the remission of sin.

For God so loved the world that He gave His only begotten Son that whoever believes in Him and not just Him but also in His name will not perish but have eternal life. Having eternal life with God is to spend eternity with Him. He sent His Son that whoever receives Him has a right to become children. Heirs of God and joint heirs with Christ.

Jesus the Christ came to destroy the works of the devil. He also came that we may have life and the abundance of life. That we may have life not only in this world but also in the world to come.

Romans 5:1 *Being therefore justified by faith; we have peace with God through our Lord Jesus Christ.* _{WEB}

HiS SPiRiT

He Is Spirit
Saving Promise Is Real In Truth

Jesus Promises the Holy Spirit

Have you received the Holy Spirit? Have you heard of the Holy Spirit? As Paul was passing by other disciples in a certain town, Scripture found in Acts 19:2-7 He said to them, *"Did you receive the Holy Spirit when you believed?" They said to him, "No, we haven't even heard that there is a Holy Spirit". He said, "Into what then were you baptized?" They said, "Into John's baptism. Paul said, "John indeed baptized with the baptism of repentance, saying to the people that they should believe in the one who would come after him, that is, in Jesus." When they heard this, they were baptized in the name of the Lord Jesus. When Paul had laid his hands on them, the Holy Spirit came on them, and they spoke with other languages and prophesied. There were about twelve men in all.* WEB

John 14:15-25 *If you love Me, keep My commandments. I will pray to the Father, and **He will give you another Counselor, that He may be with you forever, the Spirit of Truth**, whom the world cannot receive; for it does not see Him, neither knows Him. You know Him, for **He lives with you, and will be in you. I will not leave you orphans.** I will come to you. Yet a little while, and the world will see Me no more; but you will see Me. Because I live, you will live also. In that day you will know that I am in My Father, and you in Me, and I in you. One who has My commandments, and keeps them, that person is one who loves Me. One who loves Me will be loved by My Father, and I will love Him, and will reveal Myself to him." Judas (not Iscariot) said to Him, "Lord, what has happened that You are about to reveal Yourself to us, and not to the world?" Jesus answered him, "If a man loves Me, he will keep My word. My Father will love him, and We will come to him, and make Our home with him. He who does not love Me does not keep My words. The word which you hear is not Mine, but the Father's who sent Me. I* *have said these things to you, while still living with you. But **the Counselor, the Holy Spirit, whom the Father will send in My name, He will teach you all things, and will remind you of all that I said to you.*** <small>WEB</small>

Once we receive Christ, He will seal His Spirit in us.

Ephesians 4:30 tells us ***do not grieve the Holy Spirit*** *of God, in whom you were sealed for the day of redemption.* What is redemption? Scripture tells us that Christ has redeemed us from the law of sin and death. He has purchased us with His own blood. Therefore, we have been bought with a price. The price was the precious blood of Jesus Christ. Christ is the mediator of the new covenant because He died for us. Now the believers are sealed with the promise which is His Holy Spirit. One day Jesus is coming back for us. This is the Spirit of Promise spoken of throughout Scripture according to 2 Corinthians 5:5 *Now He who prepared us for this very purpose is God, who gave to us the Spirit as a pledge.* <small>WEB</small>

Our Father in Heaven gives His children the Holy Spirit to those who want to know Him found in Luke 11:13 *If you then, being evil, know how to give good gifts to your children, **how much more will your heavenly Father give the Holy Spirit to those who ask Him?*** <small>WEB</small>

God Gave His Spirit mentioned in Acts 5:32 *And we are witnesses of these things; and so is the Holy Spirit, whom God has given to those who obey Him.* <small>WEB</small>

Ephesians 4:30 *Don't grieve the Holy Spirit of God, in whom you were sealed for the day of redemption.* <small>WEB</small>

His Spirit is sealed in every believer, we must not grieve

His Spirit. We grieve His Spirit by not giving Him free access to our lives. We grieve Him when we confine Him to one or only a few areas in our lives instead of giving Him free access to every area. We do this when we pick and choose which areas, we will give Him access to. The Holy Spirit is a Gentleman He will not force His will or way. His Spirit will unction us what to do and what not to do. The Holy Spirit will send us, redirect us, and stop us in our tracks. He will even unction us what to say, and what not to say. He will unction us when to say something and when not to say anything. Will also unction us where to say it and even how to say it. He will even unction us to be quiet. That brief pause before we speak is His unction. His unction's is the anointing; it is the oil that flows through the believer to keep us in line with God's will for our lives. The more we obey the Holy Spirit the more the flow of God flows through us. Many times, we push right past His unction and block the flow.

As it is mentioned the Holy Spirit is a Gentleman and He will not make us obey Him. God gave all of us a free will choice. His Spirit will allow room for the free will God gave to us. His Spirit will bring to our remembrance all the things Jesus taught. His Spirit will lead us, guide us, comfort us, protect us, make intercessions for us and much more. When the Holy Spirit is in operation, we will need of no one to teach us, the Spirit we receive will teach us all things because He is real and not counterfeit. All we must do is obey. In 1 John 2:27 *As for you, the anointing which you received from Him remains in you, and you do not need for anyone to teach you. But as His anointing teaches you concerning all things, and is true, and is no lie, and even as it taught you, you will remain in Him.* WEB

In the World English Bible 2 Timothy 2:15 **Give diligence to present yourself approved by God,** *a worker who does not need to be ashamed, properly handling the* <u>Word of Truth</u>.

Let us open this book to see some of the obstacles in one's life that may try to hinder us from reaching all that God has for us.

INTRODUCTION

In life we have many obstacles to keep us from reaching our goals or God's purpose for our lives. The Holy Scripture tells us that all things work together according to *Romans 8:28 We know that all things work together for good for those who love God, to those who are called according to his purpose.* WEB

We will find that love and forgiveness play a particularly key role in our healing. There are some deeply rooted issues that we may or may not be aware of standing in our way. In this book we will be dealing briefly with various areas of obstacles that may play a vital role in us not being able to break through those barriers.

When one desire is to no longer be stuck behind a wall blocking out God. We must break down that wall brick by brick and layer by layer. God's Word is the solid foundation on which we build our house on. Our house is our temple that belongs to God. Our temple which is our body that we are to offer to God according to Romans 12:1 *we are to present our bodies a living sacrifice, holy, acceptable to God, which is your spiritual service.* WEB

We want to Give God, His Son and His Holy Spirit free will access to all of us in every area of our lives. There are so many areas that we hold on to and are not willing to allow anyone in those sections. There are also spots that we are unaware of in our own lives. Although we may not be able to tackle all of them, once we recognize a few areas we can begin. Once we begin to allow God who is the Potter, to mold and make us because we are His clay.

Jesus is the foundation on which we began to build, He will break up all the fallow ground so we can build on a sturdy foundation. Tearing down the walls we have built without escape routes. We must build our house on a firm substructure. Rebuilding a house of love, forgiveness and much more from the ground up. Breaking generations of things, knowing whose you are and who you belong to. In our house we have doors and windows which are our gateways. When we shut them, we not only shut others out we shut God out. Jesus wants us to open the door for Him Scripture found in Revelation 3:20 inside the World English Bible Jesus said *Behold, I stand at the door and knock. If anyone hears My voice and opens the door, then I will come in to him, and will dine with him, and he with Me.* Jesus said He stand at the door and knock. Jesus knocks at the door of our hearts. We do not want to leave Him standing there knocking. When you hear His voice let Him in.

We know that every day will not be perfect but we have a perfect Father in Heaven who will be there with us. His Word tells us that all things work together for our good and according to His purpose.

In this book we will be dealing in short with the mind, will, emotions, body, flesh, spirit, heart, soul as well as other areas. We will see how all these areas tie in with God, His love and forgiveness. Also, how we must share the love towards God and towards one another.

All of God's Scriptures are important. I used capital letters and bold letters only to emphasize in relation to the topic discussion.

Love

GOD IS LOVE (1 JOHN 4:16)

Love Opens Various Emotions
And
Looks Over Various Emotions

Although love is affiliated with our emotional side it is much more than just emotions. Love is a word many people use all too loosely. The word love requires a selfless action. Yes! Love is an action word therefore love is not just a word we say, love is what we display.

Love is a word often misused or taken lightly. Many relate this word to how someone makes them feel at the moment. Sometimes it is used based on what the person has done. One will say they love someone based on financial, physical, emotional, or spiritual provision. However, when they can longer meet or satisfy that need, they no longer love the person or are not in love with that person anymore.

There is a difference between love and falling in love. Anything we can fall into we can fall out of. Notice the Holy Scripture never uses the words falling in love. The Word of God used love. According to His Word love looks over various emotions 1 Corinthians 13:8 Love never fail. If we ever genuinely loved someone and even if it did not work there will still be love there. After you have gone through the hurt and the pain once you have learned how to honestly forgive them. That love will remain but it will just be put in its proper place.

Very few people know what it really means to love. Some people mistake lust for love. True love comes from God because God is love. The dictionary has a meaning of love, the world has a meaning of love and God's word truly has the true meaning of love. God's love is found in John 3:16 *For God so loved the world, that He gave His one and only Son, that whoever believes in Him should not perish, but have eternal life.* WEB

The book of Romans chapter five verse eight shares with us the demonstration of God's love *But God commends His own love toward us, in that while we were yet sinners, Christ died for us.* WEB

What kind of love does God want us to have in our lives? He wants us to experience and express the kind of love like what is described in 1 Corinthians 13:4-7 a love that's patient, kind and much more.

When we have fully experienced that kind of love. That is the perfect love that will cast out or expel all fear according to1 John 4:18.

Why is it important to know the love of God? It is important to know the kind of love that nothing can separate us from His love as stated in Romans 8:35-39.

Why is it important to God for His children to experience such a love in Him? Love comes from God and let us look at 1 John 4:7-21 ***Beloved, let us love one another, for love is of God; and everyone who loves is born of God, and knows God.*** *He who does not love does not know God, for God is love. By this God's love was revealed in us, that God has sent His one and only Son into the world that we might live through Him.* ***In this is love, not that we loved God, but that He loved us,*** *and sent His Son as the atoning sacrifice for our sins.* ***Beloved, if God loved us in this way, we also ought to love one another.*** *No one has seen God at any time. If we love one another, God remains in us, and His love has been perfected in us. By this we know that we remain in Him and He in us, because He has given us of His Spirit. We have seen and testify that the Father has sent the Son as the Savior of the world. Whoever confesses that Jesus is the Son of God, God remains in Him, and He in God. We know and have believed the love which God has for us.* ***God is love,*** *and he who remains in love remains in God, and God remains in him. In this love has been made perfect among us, that we may have boldness in the day of judgment, because as He is, even so are we in this world.* ***There*** *is no fear in love; but perfect love casts out fear because fear has punishment. He who fears is not made perfect in love.* **We love Him because He first loved us.** *If a man says, "I love God," and hates his brother, he is a liar; for he who does not love his brother whom he has seen, how can he love God whom he has not seen?* **This commandment we have from Him, that he who loves God should also love his brother** *and sister.* _{WEB}

1 John 3:16-18 *By this we know love, because He laid down His life for us. And we ought to lay down our lives for the brothers* and sisters. *But whoever has the world's goods and sees his* or her *brother* or sister *in need, then closes his* or her *heart of compassion against Him,* **how does God's love remain in him** or her? **My little children, let us not love in word only, or with the tongue only, but indeed and truth.** _{WEB}

They will know that we belong to God and are His disciples by the love, we have one for another. We must love not only in words but in actions and deeds. Amen!

Looking for love can be an obstacle too. When we are looking for love in all the wrong places we can end up with the same spirit with a different face.

We must live in God's purpose on purpose: WE MUST LOVE GOD, LOVE YOURSELF AND LOVE EVERYONE AS WE LOVE OURSELVES in Mark 12:30-31. YES! We must even love our enemies in Matthew 5:44. Let us make a godly choice to MAKE PEACE WITH ALL found in Matthew 6:9; Romans 14:19; and James 3:18.

We are not to let our natural affections get in the way of our love and obedience to our Heavenly Father. Our Father in Heaven loves us and likewise we are to love Him with everything within us.

CHAPTER 2

Battles and Wars

Battles Always Try To Legalize Every Stronghold
And
Warfare Always Release Strongholds

WE ALL HAVE BATTLES OF THE MIND

We cannot fight these battles in our mind alone or in the flesh according to 2 Corinthians 10:4-6 *for **the weapons of our warfare is not of the flesh, but mighty before God** to the throwing down of strongholds, throwing down imaginations and every high thing that is exalted against the knowledge of God and bringing every thought into captivity to the obedience of Christ, and being in readiness to avenge all disobedience when your obedience is made full.* WEB

When we do not cast these battles down, they become strongholds in our mind. These strongholds are obstacles that stop or hinder us early in the process long before we even begin to progress. They are called strongholds because they have a strong hold on our minds which affects our whole body. This will try to keep us from reaching our full obedience in God. Our mind must be transformed and renewed in Christ. The way we think is the way a person becomes. Therefore, we must guard our heart and mind.

THE ENEMY WANTS CONTROL AND HE USES MANY TACTICS such as fears, doubt, worry, unbelief, false doctrine and more (2 Corinthians 2:11; 2 Corinthians 4:4; Ephesians 6:11). He uses the same three tactics found in 1 John 2:16 "The lust of the flesh, the lust of the eyes and the pride of life." All that comes from the world and not from our Father in heaven. These tactics primarily work on the individuals who are tempted. Why? Because we are tempted BY THAT VERY THING WE WANT or want to do. When we are tempted, we are drawn away, enticed and baited by the enemy after what we lust and desire for according to James 1:14. The things we lust and desire are all personal for everyone. Each person is tempted the same three ways. The temptations only look different because we all have different issues. We may even have different or the same lusts and desires. However, the enemy will not use what is not effective. He only uses what may be effective, even if it does not work the first time he will come back again. James 4:7 in the World English Bible tells us to *be subject therefore to God. But resist the devil, and he will flee from you.*

Many minds are blinded by the enemy so they will not believe the gospel according to 2 Corinthians 4:4 *in whom the god of this world has blinded the minds of the unbelieving, that the light of the gospel of the glory of Christ, who is the image of God, should not dawn on them.* WEB

GOD WANTS OUR MIND AND NOT JUST OUR MIND BUT ALL OF US. HE ALSO HAS GIVEN US A FREE WILL CHOICE. Isaiah 26:3-4 *You will keep whoever's mind is steadfast in perfect peace, because he* or she *trusts in You. Trust in Yahweh forever; for in Yah, Yahweh, is an everlasting Rock.* WEB

According to the Holy Scriptures in the World English Bible *You shall love the Lord your God with all your heart, with all your soul, and with all your mind.* (Matthew 22:37; Mark 12:30; Luke 10:27) PEOPLE WANT CONTROL of our minds: Psalm 1:1-4 *Blessed is the man who does not walk in the counsel of the wicked.* It does not matter who they are if their counsel is ungodly or unbiblical it is ungodly counsel. *nor stand on the path of sinners.* Do not stand in the way of sinners. *nor sit in the seat of scoffers.* Do not join in with the ones mocking others neither should you mock or be little anyone *but His delight is in Yahweh's law. On His law he meditates day and night. He will be like a tree planted by the streams of water, that produces its fruit in its season, whose leaf also does not wither. Whatever he does shall prosper. The wicked are not so, but are like the chaff which the wind drives away.* WEB

WE WANT CONTROL of our own minds: Philippians 4:6-7 *In nothing be anxious, but in everything, by prayer and petition with thanksgiving, let your requests be made known to God. And the peace of God, which surpasses all understanding, will guard your hearts and your thoughts in Christ Jesus.* WEB

1 CORINTHIANS 6:19-20 *Or do you not know that your body is a temple of the Holy Spirit who is in you, whom you have from God? You are not your own, for you were bought with a price. Therefore, glorify God in your body and in your spirit, which are God's.* WEB

Jesus paid the sin debt He purchased us with His own blood on the cross. We not only have battles of the mind we have wars going on within. Wars that lead us into tug of war between our flesh and spirit.

We must have the attitude of Christ according to Philippians 2:5-11 *Have this in your mind, which was also in Christ Jesus, who, existing in the form of God, did not consider equality with God a thing to be grasped, **but emptied Himself, taking the form of a servant**, being made in the likeness of men. And being found in human form, **He humbled Himself, becoming obedient to death, yes, the death of the cross.*** WEB

We must keep our minds focused on God. The trials we face are necessary so that we are complete in Him and are lacking nothing. Scripture tells us if we lack wisdom, we must ask God. James 1:2-8 *Count it all joy, my brothers,* and sisters, *when you fall into various temptations, **knowing that the testing of your faith produces endurance. Let endurance have its perfect work, that you may be perfect and complete, lacking in nothing. But if any of you lacks wisdom, let him** or her ask of God, who gives to all liberally and without reproach; and it will be given to him or her. But let him or her ask in faith, without any doubt, for he or she who doubts is like a wave of the sea, driven by the wind and tossed. For let that man or woman not think that he will receive anything from the Lord. He is a double-minded man or woman, unstable in all his ways.* WEB

When many of the Scriptures say man, it is referring to humankind.

We must not be double-minded. Being double-minded causes us to be unstable. Unstable in not just one way or area of our life but in ALL of them. When we do not deal with those battles in our mind. Those battles in our mind seep down to our heart. Out of our heart flows the issues of life. Our heart ponders many things. Remember Scripture tells us above all the heart is deceitful and desperately wicked. Unless our heart has been cleansed and we are renewed with the right spirit daily. In Psalm 51:10 of the World English Bible David said *Create in me a clean heart, O God. Renew a right spirit within me.* _{WEB}

We all have battles in our mind and if we do not cast them down with the spiritual weapons through God. Anything contrary to God's Word we must cast down with God's Word. We must protect our minds. Ephesians 6:17 tells us *to put on the helmet of the salvation.* _{WEB}

If our mind is not transformed and renewed, we will not even know how to demonstrate what is good and pleasing to God to do His will. Romans 12:2 *Don't be conformed to this world, but be **transformed by the renewing of your mind**, so that you may prove what is the good, well-pleasing, and perfect will of God.* _{WEB}

People have said that one is so heavenly minded they are no earthly good. This saying is contrary to Scripture. In fact, you do not even see verses like that in the Word of God. Colossians 3:2 Tell us to ***Set your mind on the things that are above***, *not on the things that are on the earth.* _{WEB}

There is a war going on within and these wars are between the flesh and the spirit. We all have a human spirit that is spelled with a lower-case "s". The believers have both the human spirit and the Holy Spirit that is spelled with a capital "S". When we have a war between the flesh and the spirit it pulls our soul (mind, will, emotions) towards whichever one is ruling. If the flesh is in control, then your soul will follow and be ruled by the body. If your spirit is in control then your soul will follow and be led by the Spirit. Remember our soul is our mind, will and emotions. Therefore, whether we are body ruled or spirit ruled. There is a war going on within the members of our body according to Romans 7:21 and when we desire to do good evil is still present.

When there is so much going on in our minds we still must pray, fast, study, meditate and more. Paraphrasing Isaiah 26:3 *You will keep whoever's mind is steadfast in perfect peace, because they trust in You.* We must think on Godly thoughts and cast down all those lofty thought's contrary to the Word of God. We must humble ourselves as a child of God and serve Him. Remember in everything give God thanks this is His will for us in Christ Jesus.

CHAPTER 3

Be filleD WiTH RiGHT FRUiTS

Fruit Relates Us In The Spirit

What are some of the good and bad fruit we can be filled with?

There are fruitless deeds because they are works of the flesh. We are not to fulfill the lust of the flesh. Fulfilling the lust of the flesh do not bear Godly fruit. Since it does not bear Godly fruit, it is considered fruitless.

Galatians 5:19-21 *Now the deeds of the flesh are obvious, which are: adultery, sexual immorality, uncleanness, lustfulness, idolatry, sorcery, hatred, strife, jealousies, outbursts of anger, rivalries, divisions, heresies, envy, murders, drunkenness, orgies, and things like these; of which I forewarn you, even as I also forewarned you, that those who practice such things will not inherit God's Kingdom.* WEB

We have been forewarned and whatever is written before is written for our learning.

There is spiritual fruit that God wants us to have to crucify the flesh. These fruits are found in Galatians 5: 22-26 *But the fruit of the Spirit is love, joy, peace, patience, kindness, goodness, faith, gentleness, and self-control. Against such things there is no law. Those who belong to Christ have crucified the flesh with its passions and lusts. If we live by the Spirit, let us also walk by the Spirit. Let us not become conceited, provoking one another, and envying one another.* WEB

We must think on pure thoughts. Therefore, if we think on these things according to the Holy Scripture, found in Philippians 4:8 *Finally, brothers and sisters, whatever things are true, whatever things are honorable, whatever things are just, whatever things are pure, whatever things are lovely, whatever things are of good report: if there is any virtue and if there is any praise, think about these things.* <small>WEB</small>

We must no longer walk in the deceitfulness of our own mind and hearts. Above all the heart is deceitful and desperately wicked and who can truly know our heart and mind but God. Our hearts and minds must be renewed in Yeshua Ha Mashiach/Jesus the Christ.

There is a way that seems right to humanity but to the end leads death and destruction (Proverb 14:13 & 16:25). Everyone thinks they are right in their own eyes but God weighs the heart (Proverb 21:2). Once we receive Christ and our desire should become more to please Him though our obedience to Him. We will no longer lack understanding and be detached from the life of God due to our own ignorance or the hardness of our heart. Because we will no longer walk in darkness with blinded minds. We will become new in Him and the old things passed away BECAUSE WE BECOME A NEW CREATION IN HIM. We are to no longer give ourselves-up to sensuality and greediness of any kind. Nor to any impure action or practice. WE MUST PRESENT OUR BODIES A LIVING SACRIFICE UNTO GOD WHICH IS A REASONABLE SERVICE TO HIM. After all Christ is who came to give us a new life. Once we have heard about Him, we must take up His Yoke and learn from Him as stated in Matthew 11:29 World English Bible *Take My yoke upon you, and learn from Me, for I am gentle and lowly in heart; and you will find rest for your souls.*

When working in the fruit of the spirit we must continue seeking the Father daily for rest for your mind, will and emotion.

Scripture tells us to taste and see that the Lord is good. I learned in medical school that digestion begins in the mouth. Eat His Word and drink His Word daily. The only way you can get this fruit is through Jesus.

CHAPTER 4

HUNGRY AND THIRSTY

Psalm 42:1 As the deer pants for the water brooks, so my soul pants after You, God. My soul thirsts for God, for the living God. When shall I come and appear before God. _{WEB}

When a deer is panting for the water brooks, it is more than thirsty for a drink it is panting for its life. Also, it is not only thirsty for its life it is trying to escape. The water helps the deer by causing the hunter to lose track of its scent. The water is vital in the protection of its survival. The very life of the deer depends not only on finding the water but drinking it. The water is all around it and inside it. Just like our life depends on the True and Living God. His Spirit is the water that we need in us and all around us. This is the way our soul must thirst for God.

Everyone is hungry and thirsty for something. What is it that you are hungry and thirsty for?

Jesus wants us to be hungry and thirsty for Him and His righteousness.

In John 6:54 Jesus said *He who eats My flesh and drinks My blood **has eternal life**, and I will raise him up at the last day.* _{WEB}

He did not mean eat His flesh and drink His blood. Jesus declared, whoever comes to Me will never go hungry, and whoever believes in Me will never be thirsty.

In the Old Testament God allowed it to rain down manna from heaven for the children of Israel in the wilderness. Jesus is the bread of life that came down from heaven. Man should not live by natural bread alone but every word that continues out of the mouth of God.

11

Life of the flesh is in the blood, and the Lord gave Himself to make amends for our souls. It is by His life that is in the blood that makes amends. A blood covenant, which He poured out for many for the forgiveness of sins.

At the last supper Jesus used wine as a representation of His blood. In Matthew 26:26-29 *As they were eating, Jesus took bread, gave thanks for it, and broke it. He gave to the disciples, and said, "Take, eat; this is My body." He took the cup, gave thanks, and gave to them, saying, "All of you drink it, for this is My blood of the new covenant, which is poured out for many for the remission of sins. But I tell you that I will not drink of this fruit of the vine from now on, until that day when I drink it anew with you in My Father's Kingdom.* WEB

Jesus' new wine He leaves with us is His Holy Spirit. Ephesians 5:18 *Do not be drunken with wine, in which is dissipation, but be filled with the Spirit.* WEB

We must not be thirsty for natural wine and spirits (strong drink) but thirst for the Spirit of God. We are not to be filled with natural wines but filled with His Spirit.

We must come to Him hungry and thirsty. We have spent most of our lives filling up on the fruitless deeds in life. We really do not know if we are hungry and thirsty until we reach a spiritual famine in our lives. Therefore, we must empty ourselves and allow God to empty us of all the junk we have accumulated throughout the years. Then once we are empty allow Jesus to fill us with His Spirit so we can develop the fruits of the Spirit. When we are filled with the fruits of the Spirit will begin to develop His characteristics. The characteristics that He wants us to have. Once we have lost the desire for the worldly or physical things and gain the desire for spiritual things. Then our appetite will change, our desires and cravings will be more for Him.

Let us read the Scripture about the woman at the well found in John 4:1-42 of the World English Bible. *Therefore, when the Lord knew that the Pharisees had heard that Jesus was making and baptizing more disciples than John (although Jesus Himself did not baptize, but (His disciples), He left Judea and departed into Galilee. He needed to pass through Samaria. So, He came to a city of Samaria, called Sychar, near the parcel of ground that Jacob gave to his son, Joseph. Jacob's well was there. Jesus therefore, being tired from His journey, sat down by the well. It was about the sixth hour. A woman of Samaria came to draw water. Jesus said to her, "Give me a drink." For His disciples had gone away into the city to buy food. The Samaritan woman therefore said to Him, "How is it that You, being a Jew, ask for a drink from me, a Samaritan woman?" (For Jews have no dealings with Samaritans.)* **Jesus answered her, "If you knew the gift of God, and who it is who says to you, 'Give Me a drink, you would have asked Him, and He would have given you living water."** *The woman said to Him, "Sir, you have nothing to draw with, and the well is deep. So where do you get that living water? Are you greater than our father, Jacob, who gave us the well and drank from it himself, as did his children and his livestock?"* **Jesus answered her, "Everyone who drinks of this water will thirst again, <u>but whoever drinks of the water that I will give him will never thirst again; but the water that I will give him will become in him a well of water springing up to eternal life.</u>"** *The woman said to Him, "Sir, give me this water, so that I don't get thirsty, neither come all the way here to draw." Jesus said to her, "Go, call your husband, and come here." The woman answered, "I have no husband." Jesus said to her, "you said well, I have no husband, for you have had five husbands; and he whom you now have is not your husband. This you have said truly." The woman said to Him, "Sir, I perceive that You are a Prophet. Our fathers worshiped in this mountain, and you Jews say that in Jerusalem is the place where people ought to worship." Jesus said to her, "Woman, believe Me, the hour comes, when neither in this mountain, nor in Jerusalem, will you worship the Father. You worship that which you do not know. We worship that which we know; for salvation is from the Jews.* **But the hour comes, and now is, when the true worshipers will worship the Father in spirit and truth, for the Father seeks such to be His worshipers. God is Spirit, and those who worship Him must worship in spirit and truth."** *The woman said to him, "<u>I know that Messiah comes, He who is called Christ. When He has come, He will declare to us all things.</u>" Jesus said to her, "**<u>I am He, the One who speaks to you.</u>**" At this, His disciples came. They marveled that He was speaking with a woman; yet no one said, "What are you looking for?"*

or, "Why do you speak with her?" So, the woman left her water pot, went away into the city, and said to the people, "Come, see a Man who told me everything that I did. Can this be the Christ?" They went out of the city, and were coming to Him. **In the meanwhile, the disciples urged Him, saying, "Rabbi, eat." But He said to them, "I have food to eat that you don't know about." The disciples therefore said to one another, "Has anyone brought Him something to eat?" Jesus said to them, "My food is to do the will of Him who sent Me and to accomplish His work.** *Don't you say, 'There are yet four months until the harvest?' Behold, I tell you, lift up your eyes and look at the fields, that they are white for harvest already. He who reaps receives wages and gathers fruit to eternal life; that both he who sows and he who reaps may rejoice together. For in this the saying is true, 'One sows, and another reaps.' I sent you to reap that for which you have not labored. Others have labored, and you have entered into their labor." From that city many of the Samaritans believed in Him because of the word of the woman, who testified, "He told me everything that I did." So, when the Samaritans came to Him, they begged Him to stay with them. He stayed there two days.* **Many more believed because of His word. They said to the woman, "Now we believe, not because of your speaking; for we have heard for ourselves, and know that this is indeed the Christ, the Savior of the world."**

We must have that hunger and thirst after righteousness as we had in unrighteous. Just as much or more than we had when we were in the world. He called us out of darkness into His amazing light. He did not make a mistake. He wants to use us for His glory.

According to Scripture Jesus said to the fishermen come let Me make you fishers of men. Therefore, when He called or chose us, He knew exactly who He selected and why He picked the individual. In John 6:70-71 *Jesus answered them,* **"Didn't I choose you, the twelve, and one of you is a devil?"** *Now He spoke of Judas, the son of Simon Iscariot, for it was he who would betray Him, being one of the twelve* and when Jesus prayed to the Father in John 17:12 *While I was with them in the world, I kept them in Your name. Those whom You have given Me I have kept.* **None of them is lost, except the son of destruction, that the Scripture might be fulfilled.** WEB

Remember what you were in the world. He will use that and show us a new way of doing it. The new way is His way. Here are a few examples: If you were a fighter in the streets, He wants you to fight in the Spirit through prayer, intercession, spiritual warfare. If you were a drinker, He wants you to be drunk in the Spirit. Put down the natural wine and spirit and drink the Word of God. It is that same energy you had when you were on the enemy's side. That same kind of hunger, thirst and more now that you are on the Lord's side.

When we hunger and thirst after His righteousness, He will fill us with righteousness. Jesus will help us put off the old sinful nature of corruption through our deceitful desires, to be renewed in the spirit of our minds, and to put on the new self, true righteousness, and holiness after the likeness of God.

Once we are hungry and thirsty enough like the deer that pants for the water. HE WILL SHOW US OURSELVES; He will reveal Himself to us. He will fill us with a new hunger and thirst for Him, that we will no longer hunger and thirst after what the world and our flesh have to offer.

CHAPTER 5

GOOD FRUIT BAD FRUIT

In Genesis 1:12 the concept of the tree and its seed *the earth brought forth vegetation, plants* **yielding seed after their kind, and trees bearing fruit with seed in them, after their kind;** *and God saw that it was good* ᴡᴇʙ.

In Matthew 7:16 –20 Jesus says **by their fruits you will know them.** *Do you gather grapes from thorns, or figs from thistles? Even so,* **every good tree produces good fruit; but the corrupt tree produces evil fruit. A good tree cannot produce evil fruit, neither can a corrupt tree produce good fruit.** *Every tree that does not grow good fruit is cut down, and thrown into the fire. Therefore,* **by their fruits you will know them.** ᴡᴇʙ

John 15 World English Bible Jesus is the True Vine. Starting at verse *1 I am the true Vine, and My Father is the Farmer. 2* **Every branch in Me that does not bear fruit, He takes away. Every branch that bears fruit, He prunes, that it may bear more fruit.** *3 You are already pruned clean because of the word which I have spoken to you. 4 Remain in Me, and I in you.* **As the branch cannot bear fruit by itself, unless it remains in the Vine, so neither can you, unless you remain in Me. 5 I am the Vine, you are the branches. He who remains in Me, and I in him, the same bears much fruit, for apart from me you can do nothing.** *6 If a man* **does not remain in Me, he is thrown out as a branch, and is withered**; *and they gather them, throw them into the fire, and they are burned. 7 If you remain in Me, and My words remain in you, you will ask whatever you desire, and it will be done for you. 8* **In this is My Father glorified, that you bear much fruit; and so, you will be My disciples.** *9 Even as the Father has loved Me, I also have loved you. Remain in My love. 10 If you keep My commandments, you will remain in My love; even as I have kept My Father's commandments, and remain in His love. 11 I have spoken these things to you, that My joy may remain in you, and that your joy may be made full.12 This is My commandment, that you love one another, even as I have loved you.*

Proverb 11:30-31 *The fruit of the righteous is a tree of life. He who is wise wins souls.* *Behold, the righteous shall be repaid in the earth; how much more the wicked and the sinner!* _{WEB}

John 15:16 World English Bible **You did not choose me, but I chose you, and appointed you, that you should go and bear fruit, and that your fruit should remain;** *that whatever you will ask of the Father in My name, He may give it to you.*

CHAPTER 6

TWO KINDS

We are told to go bear fruit but there are two kinds of fruit. The two kinds are righteous and unrighteous There are two kinds of people lost and saved (Matthew 13:24-30; Matthew 25:31-46). Let us look at what Scripture has to say about this. According to Ephesians 2:8-9 *for by grace you have been saved through faith, and that not of yourselves; it is the gift of God, not of works, that no one would boast* (Read full chapter). WEB We must go bear fruit after our own kind, we were once lost and now by grace we are saved. What are the obstacles that keep us from bearing fruit after what God has delivered us from? Is it sin, fear, selfishness, doubt, lack of faith, shame? We must go to God because he did not deliver us just for ourselves. He delivered us to help others get delivered. Did you know one water and one plant but it is God who gives the increase? We may either water or plant He gives the increase to His Kingdom.

What kind of fruits are both found in Galatians chapter five? Work of the flesh which is fruitless: "adultery, sexual immorality, uncleanness, lustfulness, idolatry, sorcery, hatred, strife, jealousies, outbursts of anger, rivalries, divisions, heresies, envying, murders, drunkenness and orgies. Fruit of the spirit is love, joy, peace, patience, kindness, goodness, faith, gentleness and self-control."

Jesus came from heaven to earth to save us and show us the right way. Luke 19:10 *For the Son of Man came to seek and to save that which was lost* WEB.

Either we believe or do not believe according to Mark 16:16 *He who believes and is baptized will be saved; but he who disbelieves will be condemned.* WEB

If we are dead to sin and then we are alive to God. Therefore, we are not to continue in sin, we are baptized in Christ's death and buried by baptism into His death. Just as He was raised from the dead by the Heavenly Father we are resurrected into a new life.

Once we receive Him, we are now children in the newness of life. We will one day be with Him forever. We are heirs of God and joint heirs with Christ. United with Christ so we will no longer be a slave to sin. Therefore, we should not continue in sin once we die to it and rise into the newness of life.

Yes, we all fall short of God's glory. If anyone says they have no sin they are a liar. We are under God's grace but grace is not a license to let sin reign and rule over us.

Romans 6:1-2 *What shall we say then? Shall we continue in sin, that grace may abound?* **May it never be!** *We who died to sin, how could we live in it any longer?* WEB

It is by God's grace which is His unmerited favor. Read Romans chapter 6 about God's grace and being dead to sin and alive with God. Therefore, we do not purposely continue in sin that we are under grace. Know that grace is not a license or a permit to sin as I have mentioned in the earlier paragraph. God spared us from the punishment we deserved by giving us a chance to repent and turn from sin towards God. His grace is when you get more than you deserve and God's mercy is when you do not get exactly what you deserve. He gives us space and time to repent because of His love for us.

There are two kinds of believers: spiritual and carnal (Galatians 5:17).

Sometimes carnal minded believers behave like the lost. This happens because the mind is set on fleshly and earthly things. Scripture tells us about the mind set on the flesh and a mind set on the Spirit.

The mind set on the flesh is death because it is hostile toward God but the mind set on the Spirit is life and peace according to (Romans 8:6-7)

and in Galatians 5:16-17 of the World English Bible *walk by the Spirit, and you will not fulfill the lust of the flesh. For the flesh lusts against the Spirit, and the Spirit against the flesh; and these are contrary to one another, that you may not do the things that you desire.* WEB

Carnal minded believers are friendly with the world and the world's systems. All who want to be a friend of the world make themselves an enemy of God.

Let us look at the parable of the ten virgins: five of them were wise and five of them were foolish. In Matthew twenty-five of the World English Bible verses one to thirteen. Starting at verse one *Then the Kingdom of Heaven will be like ten virgins, who took their lamps, and went out to meet the Bridegroom.*

Ten is the number of local and human governments found in Ruth 4:2 when it speaks about ten men elders of the city. What does Scripture refer to when they speak about the lamp? Let us look at Matthew 6:22 **The lamp of the body is the eye**. If therefore your eye is sound, your whole body will be full of light. Who is the Bridegroom? Jesus is the Bridegroom in many verses this is one reference Scripture found in Matthew 9:15 of the World English Bible *Jesus said to them, Can the friends of the Bridegroom mourn, as long as the Bridegroom is with them? But the days will come when the Bridegroom will be taken away from them, and then they will fast.*

Here in verse two, there is a division amongst the ten. They were divided into two groups of five. I have always been told, two is the number of witnesses. The foolish was witness to the wise and the wise was witness to the foolish. *Five of them were foolish, and five were wise. I* was also told that the number five means grace. Since Scripture says God has no respecter of person, we see here that He gave both the wise and the foolish the same amount of grace.

Which brings us to verse three saying *Those who were foolish, when they took their lamps, took no oil with them.* We have already proven the eye stands for the lamp in verse one. *Let us find out what the oil stands for here in this parable. God anointed Jesus in* Acts 10:38 *Jesus of Nazareth, how* **God anointed Him with the Holy Spirit** *and with power.* Acts 10:45 *The gift of the* **Holy Spirit** *was also poured out.* Luke 4:8 **The Spirit of the Lord is on Me, because He has anointed** *Me* 1 John 2:27 **As for you, the anointing which you received from Him remains in you.** Therefore, metaphorically the Holy Spirit stands for the oil throughout Scripture and in these verses.

We have seen in the earlier verse the foolish went watching with their natural eyes without the Holy Spirit (no oil). The wise went watching with not only their natural eyes but their spiritual eyes. They had the Holy Spirit. Therefore, it was not by their might or their power but by the Spirit of God. Watching and walking by faith and not by sight. In Acts 1:9-11 *When He had said these things, as they were looking, He was taken up, and a cloud received Him out of their sight. While they were looking steadfastly into the sky as He went, behold, two men stood by them in white clothing, who also said, You men of Galilee, why do you stand looking into the sky?* **This Jesus, who was received up from you into the sky will come back in the same way as you saw Him going into the sky.** <small>WEB</small>

The lamp being the eye of the body. The oil represents being anointed by God with His Holy Spirit through Jesus Christ. One did not have the Spirit of God and the other group had the Spirit of God. You see many times people can look like they have the Spirit of God. They can even imitate or mimic what they have seen others do. People will judge the appearance of others but it is God that knows the heart. Our heart can be deceitful and we can be fooled by our own heart. One may believe they have His Spirit based on emotions or what someone has told them. The heart is deceitful; it can fool others and even yourself but it will never ever fool God. Our heart must be renewed daily by God. When He returns, He will reveal the hidden treasures in a person's heart. <small>WEB</small>

Let us continue and look at verse four of Luke chapter twenty-five where Scripture says *but the wise took oil in their vessels with their lamps.* In 1st Peter 3:7 *giving honor to the woman, as to* **the weaker vessel.** The body is referred to as a vessel. In 2 Timothy 2:21 *If anyone therefore purges himself* or herself *from these,* **he will be a vessel** *for honor, sanctified, and suitable for the master's use, prepared for every good work.*

Now as we look a little deeper the oil was in them. They took oil in their vessels; they had the Holy Spirit. They were sealed with the Holy Spirit. According to Ephesians 1:13 *in whom you also, having heard the word of the truth, the Good News* **of your salvation--in whom, having also believed, you were sealed with the Holy Spirit of promise.** _{WEB}

Verse five states that *now while the Bridegroom delayed, they all slumbered and slept.* This could refer to a sleep in the natural, in the spiritual and even death. In many verses of Scripture Luke 8:52 being one of them is where Jesus refers to death as sleep. We read in the following Scriptures we will not all sleep as in death. 1 Corinthians 15:50-58 *Now I say this, brothers, that flesh and blood cannot inherit the Kingdom of God; neither does corruption inherit incorruption. Behold, I tell you a mystery.* **We will not all sleep, but we will all be changed,** *in a moment, in the twinkling of an eye, at the last trumpet. For the trumpet will sound, and* **the dead will be raised incorruptible, and we will be changed. For this corruptible must put on incorruption, and this mortal must put on immortality. But when this corruptible will have put on incorruption, and this mortal will have put on immortality,** *then what is written will happen: "Death is swallowed up in victory. Death, where is your sting? Hades, where is your victory? The sting of death is sin, and the power of sin is the law. But thanks be to God, who gives us the victory through our Lord Jesus Christ. Therefore, my beloved brothers, be steadfast, immovable, always abounding in the Lord's work, because you know that your labor is not in vain in the Lord.* _{WEB}

1 Thessalonians 4:13-18 *But we do not want you to be ignorant, brothers, concerning those* **who have fallen asleep,** *so that you do not grieve like the rest, who have no hope. For if we believe that Jesus died and rose again, even so* **God will bring with him those who have fallen asleep in Jesus. For this we tell you by the word of the Lord, that we who are alive, who are left to the coming of the Lord, will in no way precede those who have fallen asleep.** *For the Lord Himself will descend from heaven with a shout, with the voice of the archangel, and with God's trumpet.* **The dead in Christ will**

rise first, then we who are alive, who are left, <u>will be caught up together</u> with them in the clouds, to meet the Lord in the air. So, we will be with the Lord forever. Therefore comfort one another with these words. _{WEB}

In Matthew chapter twenty-five verse six go on to say *but at midnight there was a cry, 'Behold! The Bridegroom is coming! Come out to meet Him!'* I was told that midnight is the darkest part of the hours or the darkest part of the night. *That cry is the trumpet sound that was spoken of in 1 Corinthians and 1 Thessalonians of the previous paragraphs.*

Let us continue reading verses seven to nine. *Then all those virgins arose, and trimmed their lamps. The foolish said to the wise, 'Give us some of your oil, for our lamps are going out.' But the wise answered, saying, 'What if there isn't enough for us and you?* 1 Peter 4:18 *If it is hard for the righteous to be saved, what will happen to the ungodly and the sinner? The oil is not for us to give. The oil is the Holy Spirit and the Oil belongs to God. We are to share the gospel of Jesus Christ and when we receive Him, we receive the Holy Spirit through Him. We must be born again of the water and the Spirit. If we reject or neglect Him due to our ignorance or disobedience, He has the final say.* _{WEB}

If the eyes of the body are the light and if the eyes are single the whole body is light. If the eyes are not single and are in darkness then the whole body is full of darkness. If the body is the vessel and the Holy Spirit is the Oil in the vessels then one either you have Him or you do not. Therefore, when they trimmed the wicks which are their heart either it was full of light or full of darkness. When the wicks are trimmed for the oil flow through and saturated to be lit or remain lit. That wick is our hearts Scripture tells us that out of our hearts flows the issues of life the entire Scripture can be found in Proverbs 4:23. We must not be in self-deception by putting trust in our own heart. Jeramiah 17:9-10 *The heart is deceitful above all things, and it is exceedingly corrupt: who can know it? I, Yahweh, search the mind, I try the heart, even to give every man* (humankind) *according to his ways, according to the fruit of his doings.* _{WEB}

In verse nine the wise told the foolish *You go rather to those who sell, and buy for yourselves.* Now wait a minute how are they able to buy or sell right before the return of Christ. Revelation 1:17 says that **no one would be able to buy or to sell, unless he has that mark, the name of the beast or the number of his name** _{WEB}. *In Matthew 13:20-23 of the World English Bible What was sown on the rocky places, this is he* or she *who hears the word and immediately with joy receives it; yet he* or she *has no root in himself* or herself, *but* **endures for a while.** *When oppression or persecution arises because of the word, immediately he* or she *stumbles. What was sown among the thorns, this is he* or she **who hears the word, but the cares of this age and the deceitfulness of riches choke the word,** *and he becomes unfruitful.* **What was sown on the good ground, this is he who hears the word and understands it, who most certainly bears fruit** *and produces, some one hundred times as much, some sixty, and some thirty.*

Continue reading verses ten through thirteen, *while they went away to buy, the bridegroom came, and* **those who were ready went in with Him** *to the marriage feast, and the door was shut.* **Afterward** *the other virgins also came, saying,* **Lord, Lord, open to us.** *But* **He answered,** *most certainly I tell you,* **I do not know you.** *Watch therefore, for you do not know the day nor the hour in which the Son of Man is coming.*

In Matthew 7:21-23 *Not everyone who says to me, Lord, Lord, will enter into the Kingdom of Heaven;* **but he** *or she* **who does the will of my Father who is in heaven.** *Many will tell Me in that day, Lord, Lord, didn't we prophesy in Your name, in Your name cast out demons, and in Your name do many mighty works?* **Then I will tell them, I never knew you. Depart from Me, you who work iniquity.** _{WEB}

The time is now to be ready and live for Christ. We must live each day as if He is on His way back. Live our lives for Christ and love everyone every day as if it is our last. We do not know when He will return for us or call us to rest in sleep unto death.

CHAPTER 7

ONe

Ephesians 4:4-6 *There is **one body, and one Spirit**, even as you also were called in one hope of your calling; one **Lord, one faith, one baptism, one God and Father of all**, who is over all, and through all, and in us all.* WEB

The Holy Spirit is the One True Spirit and He is sealed in every believer. Ephesians 4:30 *Don't grieve the Holy Spirit of God, in whom you were sealed for the day of redemption.* WEB

CHRIST IS COMING BACK and when He returns, He is looking for His bride. His bride is individually a group of people and not a building. The body of believers is the one church according to Ephesians 5:27 *that He might present **the assembly** to Himself gloriously, not having spot or wrinkle or any such thing; but that **it** should be holy and without blemish.* WEB

2 Corinthians 11:22 *For I am jealous over you with a godly jealousy. For I married you to **one husband**, that I might **present you as a pure virgin to Christ.*** WEB

Therefore, the church belongs to Christ's body and is not the building made with hands not of brick, mortar, clay, wood, or such building materials. Acts 7:48 *However, the **Most High does not dwell in temples made with hands**, as the prophet says.* WEB

Therefore, the church is a living, breathing, active, body and more. The church is the body of Christ according to Romans 12:5 we are many individual members of one another who make up **one body**.

John 10:27-30 *My sheep hear My voice, and I know them, and they follow Me. I give eternal life to them. They will never perish, and no one will snatch them out of My hand. My Father, who has given them to Me, is greater than* *all. No one is able to snatch them out of My Father's hand. **I and the Father are one.*** _{WEB}

Those that leave Christ are no longer one with Him. 1 John 2:19 *They went out from us, but they did not belong to us; <u>for if they had belonged to us, they would have continued with us.</u> But they left, that they might be revealed that <u>none</u> of them belong to us.* _{WEB}

Jesus explained who His mother, sister and brother were in Matthew 12:49-50 **He stretched out His hand towards His disciples, and said, "Behold, My mother and My brothers! For whoever does the will of My Father who is in Heaven, He** or she **is My brother, and sister, and mother.** _{WEB}

In other words, we are all one who do the will of our Father in heaven There is One God, One Teacher and One Master all of us are brothers and sisters according to Matthew 23:8-12 *But do not you be called 'Rabbi,' for **One is your Teacher, the Christ**, and <u>**all** of you are brothers</u> (and sisters). Call no man on the earth your father, for **One is your Father, He who is in Heaven.** Neither be called masters, for **One is your Master, the Christ.** But he who is greatest among you will be your servant. Whoever exalts himself will be humbled, and whoever humbles himself will be exalted.* _{WEB}

Yes! We all have natural fathers, step fathers and such and there are Scriptures concerning them. However, according to this Scripture, we are all spiritual, mothers, brothers, and sisters in Christ.

God also gave some spiritual gifts in the body and they are functions and not titles. Ephesians 4:1-16 *I therefore, the prisoner in the Lord, <u>beg you to walk worthily of the calling with which you were called, with</u> all lowliness and humility, with patience, bearing with one another in love; being eager to keep the **unity of the Spirit** in the bond of peace. There is **one body, and one Spirit**, <u>even as you also **were called in one hope** of your calling; one Lord, one faith, one baptism, **one God and Father of all, who is over all, and through all**, and in us all. But to each one of us was the grace given according to the measure of the gift of Christ.</u> Therefore, He says, when He ascended on high, he led captivity captive, and **gave gifts to men.** Now this, He ascended,* *what is it but that he also first descended into the lower parts of the earth? He who descended is the one who also ascended far above all the heavens, that he might fill all things. He gave some to be* <u>*apostles; and some, prophets; and some, evangelists; and some, shepherds and teachers;*</u> **for the perfecting of the saints, to the work of serving, to the building up of the body of Christ; until we all attain to the unity of the faith, and of the knowledge of the Son of God, to a full grown man, to the measure of the stature of the fullness of Christ; we may no longer be children, tossed back and forth and carried about with every wind of doctrine, by the trickery of men, in craftiness, after the wiles of error; but speaking truth in love, we may grow up in all things into Him, who is the head, Christ; from whom all the body, being fitted and knit together through that which every joint supply, according to the working in measure of each individual part, makes the body increase to the building up of itself in love.** _{WEB}

It is not enough to only believe God is One even the demons believe He is One but they do not obey Him. We must obey God as well as believe. Yet some people still refuse to believe. Let us view what Scripture has to say in James 2:19 *You believe that* **God is One**. *You do well. The demons also believe, and shudder.* _{WEB}

Jesus's prayer for all the believers in John *17:20–21 Not for these only do I pray, but for those also who believe in Me through their word,* **that they may all be one; even as you, Father, are in Me, and I in you, that they also may be one in us;** *that the world may believe that You sent Me.* _{WEB}

1 Corinthians 12:12-27 **For as the body is one, and has many members, and all the members of the body, being many, are one body; so also, is Christ. For in one Spirit, we were all baptized into one body,** *whether Jews or Greeks, whether bond or free; and* **were all given to drink into one Spirit.** *For the* **body is not one member, but many.** *If the foot would say, "Because I'm not the hand, I'm not part of the body," it is not therefore not part of the body. If the ear would say, "Because I'm not the eye, I'm not part of the body," it is not therefore not part of the body. If the whole body were an eye, where would the hearing be? If the whole were hearing, where would the smelling be?* **But now God has set the members, each one of them, in the**

body. If they were all one member, where would the body be? **But now they are many members, but one body.** *The eye cannot tell the hand, "I have no need for you," or again the head to the feet, "I have no need for you." No, much rather, those members of the body which seem to be weaker are necessary. Those parts of the body which we think to be less honorable, on those we bestow more abundant honor; and our unpresentable parts have more abundant propriety; whereas our presentable parts have no such need. But God composed the body together, giving more abundant honor to the inferior part, that* **there should be no division in the body, but that the members should have the same care for one another. When one member suffers, all the members suffer with it. Or when one member is honored, all the members rejoice with it. Now you are the body of Christ, and members individually.** _{WEB}

We are one body with many members and we are one church. As one church we are the salt of the earth. As salt of the earth, we are strategically shaken all over the earth like salt out of a salt shaker. As salt of the salt of the earth we are not to lose our flavor according to Matthew 5:13 **You are the salt of the earth,** *but if the salt has lost its flavor, with what will it be salted? It is then good for nothing, but to be cast out and trodden under the feet of men.* _{WEB}

How do spiritual salt lose its saltiness? It loses its flavor when one gets caught up in the cares and ways of the world. According to Scripture friendship with the world is enmity with God and whoever wants to be a friend of the world makes themselves an enemy of God. Once we have lost our flavor then we become less effective in our witness for Christ. We are no longer preserved in the original state we started. Many times, one will longer desire to be a witness for Christ. One may even be using it with the wrong motives. One can be working without power and authority from on High. One can be working in one's own might and power without the Spirit of God. One can even be working in another spirit. Therefore, we will be more destructive than we are effective and will not fit for the Masters' use.

In John 8:12 *Again, therefore, Jesus spoke to them, saying,* **I am the light of the world. He who follows Me will not walk in the darkness, but will** *have the light of life.* Jesus is that light that shines through the believers. Therefore, if we are His and have His Spirit in us, we are little lights that shine in the earth. As we shine together all over the earth, we are to share that light of the gospel with others. We are the evidence that Jesus brought us out of darkness into His marvelous light. We are told to make disciples so we have a great commission to share the gospel of Jesus Christ so they can receive the light of God.

As lights we are not to forsake assembling. Wherever the believers assemble is where we gather in fellowship. Where there are two or three gathered in the name of Jesus, He will be in the mist. No matter where the location is, whether it is in a building, in a house, in the park, on a mountain or etc. For example, when Scripture talks about the church in one location or another, such as the church of Corinth they are talking about the <u>location</u>. The location where the local group came together to learn, fellowship, worship, break bread etc. When Scripture talks about the seven churches in the book of Revelation, they are giving us a description of various locations, characteristics, what good they have done and yet there is still something that He has against them. He also tells the churches what they must do to receive His promise and if they do not do what He says, what they will receive instead. All that have an ear hear what the Spirit of the Lord is saying to the churches. There is still one church but the church is in many locations doing different things.

We are to never think of ourselves more highly than we ought to. We are not to think that we have arrived when there is always room for repentance. Not everyone will come into repentance at once. Hot everyone has the same sin to repent over but we must all come into true repentance.

CHAPTER 8

CHOiCes

Christ Honors Obedience In Choices
Expecting Salvation

In life we all have choices and our choices have consequences. Scripture tells us to choose this day which God we will serve. In John Chapter one says that God sent His Word, His Word was with us, and His Word became flesh and dwelled amongst us. His Word that He sent was Jesus the Christ. God's word will not return to Him void it will accomplish wherever He sends it. If we lift up the name of Jesus, He will draw all of humankind unto Himself.

Our choices can be obstacles in our lives and even create obstacles. WE HAVE TO CHOOSE WISELY. Sometimes we make bad decisions based on our emotions. Other times based on the information we receive, advice given to us by others or plain ignorance. Other times it may be our feelings or the way we receive something. There can be many varied reasons we make wrong choices. Many times, our choice does not just affect us, it influences others too. Also, our choices can bring consequences in this life and the life to come.

Once we make our choices it is up to God how He chooses to deal with the children of obedience and the children of disobedience in Romans 9:15 Yahweh said to Moses, "I will have mercy on whom I have mercy, and I will have compassion on whom I have compassion."

HE HAS GIVEN ALL OF US ALL A FREE WILL CHOICE TO CHOOSE HIM or not to choose Him. He has given us His Word through Holy Scripture according to Romans 15:4. He has also given the believers who have received Him, His Holy Spirit through His Son

Jesus the Christ according to John 16:7. Yet! Many of the generations before us, including this generation, have forgotten Him.

Deuteronomy 5:9 says that God is Jealous and will visit the iniquity (sin) to the third and fourth generation. It is up to us to MAKE GODLY CHOICES AND break those generational curses. Those ungodly generations of traditions leading to sin and rebellion towards God our Father. Those sinful traditions that seem harmless. Those harmless things with the origin of sin that have now been accepted. They have covered up the bad roots with fables and tales, and damnable heresies (2 Peter 2:1) and doctrines of devils (1 Timothy 4:1). They try to pass them off as holy but the origin of them will never change because it's rooted and grounded in sins. Sins that God did not and do not approve of. They try to cover the truth with a lie and bury the lies by deceit.

Once we hear the truth, we have a choice to research it or to reject it. We are told that the wrath of God is revealed from heaven against all ungodliness and unrighteousness, who hold the truth in unrighteousness (Romans 1:15-18). Many will hold on to their traditions and choices with all their heart, mind, body, soul, will, emotions, flesh, spirit, and soul.

In Mark seven verse nine Jesus said in *full well do you reject the commandment of God, that you may keep your tradition.* WEB

Mark chapter seven and verse seven Jesus said *but in vain do they worship Me, teaching as doctrines the commandments of men.* WEB

Many will believe the lies hold on to them and teach them to others in ignorance. Many will know the truth and hold on to lie and make an excuse. Some even twist Scripture to compromise with the lie. Those ones that are so dear to the heart and will teach to their children and their grandchildren. Their children will teach theirs and the cycle will continue to run down the family line.

When we choose not to break and destroy those things at the root. Therefore, we choose to pass them down and carry them on to the next generation. We have no desire to break the cycle.

Many times, severing it at the root must start with us. Sometimes we do not know that we are the carrier of those things that were passed to our generations. Therefore, we can pass them down knowingly and unknowingly. In mark chapter seven verses eighteen through twenty-three Jesus said to them *are you thus without understanding also? Don't you perceive that whatever goes into the man from outside cannot defile him, because it doesn't go into his heart, but into his stomach, then into the latrine, thus purifying all foods?"* **He said, that which proceeds out of the man, that defiles the man. For _from within_, out of _the hearts_ of men, proceed evil thoughts, adulteries, sexual sins, murders, thefts, coveting, wickedness, deceit, lustful desires, an evil eye, blasphemy, pride, and foolishness. All these evil things come from within, and defile the man.** WEB

Here are some ways it is passed to our children and children's children. It may be passed down through words, actions and/or deeds. It can be passed down through either side of the family line. When it is passed down from both sides of the family line knowingly and unknowingly it may or may not be easily noticed. We pass the traditional curses down more than we pass the Word of God. Then it is left up to someone to try to break it and destroy it before it destroys us or our family. The God of the Word tells us in 1 Peter 5:5 *Likewise, your younger ones, be subject to the elder. Yes, all of you clothe yourselves with humility, to subject yourselves to one another; for "God resists the proud, but gives grace to the humble.* WEB

According to (Mark 7:13) the cycle will continue if it is not broken and destroyed. IN THIS CASE EACH PERSON IS ACCOUNTABLE FOR THEMSELVES. GENERATIONS OF DISOBEDIENCE TO GOD Paraphrasing Ezekiel 19:19-24 and 18:30 says that a soul that sins it will surely die, neither the son nor the father will bear the iniquity of one another. We must all come into true repentance. ALL SIN HAS CONSEQUENCES!

In the book of Hosea chapter four and verse six of the World English Bible *My people are destroyed for lack of knowledge. Because you have rejected knowledge, I will also reject you, that you may be no priest to me. Because you have forgotten your God's law, I will also forget your children.* WEB

According to Daniel 12:4 knowledge has increased and people will search all over for it. But they close off the Word of God and the prophecy from others to receive the true knowledge of God. Therefore, the people are perishing and destroyed for the lack of God's knowledge. Then when God's truth is introduced to them, they reject it causing themselves as well as others to move further away from the TRUTH. The truth is the laws and way of God as it is intended for His children. A new covenant not of the law written in letter with ink but the law written in our heart of the Spirit. 2 Corinthians 3:2-6 *You are our letter, written in our hearts, known, and read by all men; being revealed that you are a letter of Christ, served by us, written not with ink, but with the Spirit of the living God; not in tablets of stone, but in tablets that are hearts of flesh. Such confidence we have through Christ toward God; not that we are sufficient of ourselves, to account anything as from ourselves; but our sufficiency is from God; who also made us sufficient as servants of a new covenant; not of the letter, but of the Spirit. For the letter kills, but the Spirit gives life.* WEB

Galatians 2:16-21 *yet **knowing that a man is not justified by the works of the law but through faith in Jesus Christ, even we believed in Christ Jesus, that we might be justified by faith in Christ, and not by the works of the law, because no flesh will be justified by the works of the law.** But if, while we sought to be justified in Christ, we ourselves also were found sinners, is Christ a servant of sin? Certainly not! For if I build up again those things which I destroyed, I prove myself a law-breaker. For I, through the law, died to the law, that I might live to God. I have been crucified with Christ, and it is no longer I that live, but Christ living in me. That life which I now live in the flesh, I live by faith in the Son of God, who loved me, and gave himself up for me. I do not make void the grace of God. For if righteousness is through the law, then Christ died for nothing!* WEB

Joshua 24:15 World English Bible **If it seems evil to you to serve Yahweh, choose this day whom you will serve; whether the gods which your fathers served** that were beyond the river, or the gods of the Amorites, in whose land you dwell: **but as for me and my house, we will serve Yahweh."**

CHAPTER 9

BReaKiNG THe CURSe

Break Realizing Every Act Kept Is Not God

How do we break the curse of those things that overtake us in our lives? Interrupt those repeated cycles in our lives. Those things that keep happening in us or around us. Those times when we desire to do good but evil is still present. There are times we do not even know we are in an endless cycle.

We are not to bow down to any other gods. Bowing to gods just does not only refer to statues carved out of wood or stone. Bowing is even submitting to someone's ungodly orders. Bowing is also anything we put before our God or His Word. Then we are bowing to its meaning, we are submitting to it.

What and who are we compromising God's word for?

When we compromise too much then we are surrendering. What do we put before God? What have we made of a god? Is it that person, place, or thing in our life a big god with a little "g" becomes our capital "G" God? The Lord our God will not tolerate our love for any other gods according to His word. This is another form of worship. If we do not break or destroy this behavior or pattern at the root. We pass these things down to our children.

Let us look at Deuteronomy chapter six verse nine and ten *You shall not bow yourself down to them, nor serve them; for I, Yahweh your God, am a jealous God,* **visiting the iniquity of the fathers on the children and on the third and on the fourth generation of those who hate Me; and showing loving kindness to thousands of those who love Me and keep My commandments** (Deuteronomy 5:9-10 WEB). The Father in Heaven knows who loves and who hates Him. No matter how much we say we love Him our heart will reveal the truth. When Jesus said in Matthew 15:8 *These people draw near to Me with their mouth, and honor Me with their lips; but their heart is far from Me. And in vain do they worship Me, teaching as doctrine rules made by men.*

Many times we see repeated patterns in our family line as well as the family line of others. It is up to us to recognize what is in our generational line that has not been broken.

Take this time to pause for a moment. Pause and think of the repeated negative cycles in your own life. The ones on all sides of the families that have directly affected you and or your children.

The cycle may have skipped a few people in the family. They may be the same spirit manifested in different forms. For example, divorce and remarriages, fornication, adultery pornography, strange flesh, prostitutions or promiscuous all fall under the same or similar familiar (family) spirit. We must still love the person and hate the sin, even if we are the ones caught in a sin. We hate that sin in our own lives enough to seek Christ to be healed, deliverer and set free. We are to show no partiality to no one nor are we to be partakers in anyone's evil deeds according to Scripture.

It may have even skipped generations but it may try to rear its ugly little head, IF IT IS NOT BROKEN ENOUGH TO BE DESTROYED. It can come back in many manifestations because things broken can be fixed. However, destroyed things cannot return. We must allow Christ in to help us get rid of those ungodly things. It must be destroyed at the root.

There may even be family secrets and sins before and after you were born. Pray that it is cut off and destroyed at the root. We cannot give up, we must continue to PRAY, fast speak the truth God's truth. EVEN IF YOU RECOGNIZE IT IN SOMEONE ELSE'S FAMILY PRAY FOR THEM. We ought to pray one for another.

PRAY IN YOUR SECRET PLACE and EVEN PRAY WITH OTHERS showing love in words, actions, and deeds. We ought to tell someone that God loves them and that we love them.

Sin is poisonous as a snake it will bite you and its venom is deadly. Sin will bring forth death first spiritual death which is separation from God then eventually natural death which is eternal separation from God. In James 1:13-18 Let no man say when he is tempted, "I am tempted by God," for God cannot be tempted by evil, and He Himself tempts no one. But each one is tempted, when he is drawn away by his own lust, and enticed. **Then the lust, when it has conceived, bears sin; and the sin, when it is full grown, brings forth death**. Do not be deceived, my beloved brothers. Every good gift and every perfect gift are from above, coming down from the Father of lights, with whom can be no variation, nor turning shadow. Of His own will he brought us forth by the word of truth, that we should be a kind of first fruits of His creatures. _{WEB}

Sin is Stubborn like a mule. We know it is wrong yet it is hard to let go of sin or give it up. We must fight in prayer for ourselves and for those in sin. We must pray for our family line to be healed, delivered, and set free, pray that it does not attack another family member and pray for yourself.

When God is using someone in the family to break generational curses all hell is at war with the person God is using. Therefore, we better know whose side we are on because PLAYTIME IS OVER. YOU ARE NOT FIGHTING WITH FAMILY ANYMORE. YOU ARE COMING AGAINST ANCIENT DEMONS IN THE FAMILY LINE THAT WAS THERE LONG BEFORE YOU WERE BORN.

YOU BETTER LEARN HOW TO FIGHT and this is not a natural fight but a spiritual fight. Because any skilled fighter studies their opponents' strengths and weaknesses.

We also must know our own strengths and weaknesses. When we are weak our God is strong. We can do all things through Christ who strengthens us. Through Christ we are more than a conqueror. We can conquer those things that try to conquer us.

Most importantly we must know our heavenly Father through His Son Yeshua/Jesus. Although we know Him, He must know us or we will be operating illegally without power and authority. Let us look at the sons of Sceva found in Acts 19:11-20 *God worked special miracles by the hands of Paul, so that even handkerchiefs or aprons were carried away from his body to the sick, and the diseases departed from them, and the evil spirits went out.* ***But some of the itinerant Jews, exorcists, took on themselves to invoke over those who had the evil spirits the name of the Lord Jesus, saying, "We adjure you by Jesus whom Paul preaches.*** *There were seven sons of one Sceva, a Jewish chief priest, who did this.* ***The evil spirit answered, "Jesus I know, and Paul I know, but who are you?" The man in whom the evil spirit leaped on them, overpowered them, and prevailed against them, so that they fled out of that house naked and wounded.*** *This became known to all, both Jews and Greeks, who lived at Ephesus. Fear fell on them all, and the name of the Lord Jesus was magnified. Many also of those who had believed came, confessing, and declaring their deeds.* ***Many of those who practiced magical arts brought their books together and burned them in the sight of all. They counted their price, and found it to be fifty thousand pieces of silver. So, the word of the Lord was growing and becoming mighty.***

As we get in relationship with God and be obedient to His Word, we will become spiritually disciplined to be able to SPIRITUALLY discern. We need the Holy Spirit to be able to discern what spirit is in operation. When we know which spirit is in operation, we will know what we are dealing with and how to disarm it when we engage in spiritual warfare. We cannot even fight the strong man effectively without His Spirit. In Luke 11:21-22 *When the strong man,* ***fully armed, guards his own dwelling, his goods are safe. But when someone stronger attacks him and overcomes him, he takes from him his whole armor*** *in which he trusted, and divides his spoils.* ₩ₑᵦ

Especially, when we are breaking generational curses, we must be fully armed with Christ.

CHAPTER 10

BReak THe CYCLe

What are the cycles that need to be broken? A few of the cycles are neglect and abuse. As many of the new generations are struggling to find themselves and trying to build a healthy relationship with a significant other.

Trying to keep a roof over their head or food on the table.

Whatever it is that we are doing, we cannot keep neglecting the children. Too often in relationships many try to build broken men and women. Even if it is not a relationship it could be a career or anything the list goes on. In spending so much time in the building procedures we are breaking our children in the process, leaving them open and vulnerable. Allowing the enemy to have a foothold over them. When the enemy gets a hold, he does not want to let go without a fight. Causing this present and next generation to be affected by this. Having to find and break unknown cycles for generations to come as times gradually become worse. It is easier to build stronger children and turn our own boys into men and girls into ladies than to nurture grown people. We must end repeated cycles and it starts with you and me for this generation and the generations to come.

Let that sit right there in your spirit.

It is time to let others train our children. We have women trying to train men. We have men trying to train women. We have grandparents, aunts, uncles, siblings, friends, strangers etc. raising our children. We put them in front of the television, tablet, computer, laptops, DVD, and any electronic devices allowing them to train up our children. We have schools, daycares, baby sitters, prison systems, child protective services, institutions, the streets, and more are training many of our children.

So many of our children spend the majority of the day, evening or weekends with family or friends in the streets or in their homes. They spend a substantial part of the day in school. Many of us are working parents so we spend a lot of time away from our children whether our jobs are at home or outside of the home. So many times many people are too tired. Many parents are distracted by family, friends or trying to build new relationships.

Often when the child needs our attention, we push them away by saying later, not now, I am tired or may even yell, fuss, and curse at them. Many parents are on substance abuse or prescribed drugs to deal with their own issues in life. The others may not be on anything but it is hard for them to manage and alter everything. There are some who manage everything and hide their emotions but secretly they are a wreck. They are suffering behind their smiles and all the praises. Sometimes they are not even appreciated and they become frustrated. God knows and sees all. We can cast all our cares on Him. God wants us to be available for Him and be available for others especially our young children He loaned to us. We have a job to do when God blesses us to have children and that is to train them in Him and teach them, love, protect, nurture, discipline, encourage them and much more.

Many are abusing the children mentally, physically, emotionally knowingly and unknowingly. Some of the children are feeling neglected and rejected by their parents or guardians.

Many parents do not even know they are hanging or living with the one who is abusing the child(ren). If they have an idea they refuse to believe, may push it off as something else or leave the relationship or friendship. The abuser may be very convincing. Partially not wanting to be convinced by that unimaginable thing or not wanting to accept it for many other reasons.

We must be very mindful when the child's behaviors begin to change. Many times, their actions are misread or misunderstood. If their ways have changed due to the other person's actions, they will get into your mind first long before the child starts to show real signs. They have already begun on the child's mind prior and doing the ungodly act. Therefore, if you begin to see the behavioral changes and you ask, they may or may not tell you. If you ask them in front of the person or if the person is still in your life, they may not tell you. Depending on what the person has said to them, how the person treats you or how you feel about the person they may not tell you. Depending on your responses to situations and what they tell you they may withdraw what they have already told you. If that person is allowed to come face to face or any type of access to confront the child they may withdraw. Many times, even if you ask them, they will tell you nothing is wrong. Leaving them all alone to process whatever is going the best way they know how.

Just know that fear, hurt, and anger mimic the same or similar behaviors. Do your research and find out what those behaviors are but they are often misread. The child is accused or scolded even further damaging their spirit. When they grow up, they will still carry this hurt. Many of their hurts are due to their feelings and are rooted in fear of being neglected, abandoned, or abused in some form. There is where they have built up a wall of resistance. They want and need love but they do not trust it because the ones who are supposed to love and protect those walls have been breached. You will hear a child speak of love as if they are not loved. They will even talk about how they are hated. They will speak their hate without too many positive words. There are ones who may have learned how to deceive themselves and others for a little while but that nice guy/nice girl routine does not last exceedingly long.

When there is so much hurt in a person it opens doors for unclean spirits to enter that hurt person. I am not saying every child is possessed but there is also oppression. When a child grows into a teen or even adulthood with that hurt. Hurt people do hurt people and this supplies access to demon possession.

In delivering someone from an evil spirit we cannot medicate a demon nor can we cannot beat one out. We must cast or drive the demon out of that person. If that space is not filled with the Spirit of God it can return with more spirits and re enter that person it was expelled out according to Luke 11:24-26 *The unclean spirit,* **when he has gone out** *of the man, passes through dry places, seeking rest, and finding none,* **he says, I will turn back to my house from which I came out. When he returns, he** *finds it swept and put in order. Then he goes, and takes seven other spirits eviler than himself, and they enter in and dwell there. The last state of that man becomes worse than the first.* _{WEB}

We cannot play with this thing. It is serious and it tries to attack the young as well as the old.

In Isaiah 58:1 *Cry aloud, do not spare, lift up your voice like a trumpet, and declare to my people their disobedience, and to the house of Jacob their sins.*_{WEB}

We must break the cycle of those things that try to rob us from God. Those who try to rob God of His Glory. Those things that want to kill us and our destiny with God. Those things that will try to destroy us in this life into the next. EVEN THE FALSE TEACHINGS OF MANKIND.

Jesus said in John 10:10 of the World English Bible *the thief only comes to steal, kill, and destroy.* **I came that they may have life, and may have it abundantly.**

CHAPTER 11

WHO iS YOUR faTHeR

As much as we want to believe that everyone is a child of God. It just is not so according to Scripture. Jesus was speaking to the Pharisees in John 8:42-47 *Therefore Jesus said to them,* **If God were your Father, you would love Me, for I came out and have come from God.** *For I have not come of Myself, but He sent Me. Why don't you understand My speech? Because you cannot hear My word.* **You are of your father, the devil, and you want to do the desires of your father. He was a murderer from the beginning, and does not stand in the truth, because there is no truth in him. When he speaks a lie, he speaks on his own; for he is a liar, and the father of lies.** *But because I tell the truth, you do not believe Me. Which of you convicts Me of sin? If I tell the truth, why do you not believe Me?* **He who is of God hears the words of God or this because you do not hear, because you are not of God.** WEB

In the Previous Scripture mentioned He was not speaking of the natural father Jesus was speaking of their spiritual father the devil.

1 John 3:12 **Cain who was of the evil one,** *and killed his brother. Why did he kill him? Because his deeds were evil, and his brothers righteous.* WEB

The spirit of Cain has been running ramped all over the earth.

John 1:12-13 **But as many as received Him, to them He gave the right to become God's children, to those who believe in His name:** *who were born not of blood, nor of the will of the flesh, nor of the will of man, but of God* in Galatians chapter four verse five *states that we have been adopted in the family of God.* WEB

Galatians 4:6-7 **And because you are children, God sent out the Spirit of His Son into your hearts, crying, "Abba, Father!"** *So, you are no longer* *a bondservant, but a son; and if a son, then an heir of God through Christ. Therefore, **we are sons and daughters**.* _{WEB}

In 1 John 3 of the World English Bible verses one and two ***See how great a love the Father has given to us, that we should be called children of God!*** *For this cause the world does not know us, because it did not know Him. Beloved, now we are children of God. It is not yet revealed what we will be; but we know that when He is revealed, we will be like Him; for we will see Him just as He is.* _{WEB}

CHAPTER 12

Bear Fruit

Begin Eating All Righteous
Fruit Reach Understanding In Truth

The book of Revelation chapter two verse four encourages us to "RETURN TO our first love" He loved us first (1 John 4:19) and while we were still sinners Christ died for us (Romans 5:8). According to John 3:16 *For God so loved the world that He gave His only begotten Son that whosoever believes on Him will not perish but have everlasting life.* WEB

We did not choose Him first He chose us first. We were chosen and appointed to bear fruit (John 15:5; John 15:16). He is the vine and we are His branches in Him we are to bear fruit and without Him we cannot. We must develop the fruits of the Spirit found in Galatians 5:22-23: *love, joy, peace, patience, kindness, goodness, faithfulness, gentleness, and self-control.* WEB

We are to go bare fruit after our own kind (Genesis 11:1).

The unrighteous will not inherit the Kingdom of God (1 Corinthians 6:9-11) such were some of us but we have been washed, sanctified, justified in the name of the Lord Jesus the Christ and by the Spirit of God.

The enemy will fight tooth and nail for us to not bear fruit so we must do like Ephesians 6:10-18 says *Finally, be strong in the Lord, and in the strength of His might. Put on the whole armor of God, that you may be able to stand against the wiles of the devil. For our wrestling is not against flesh and blood, but against the principalities, against the powers, against the world's rulers of the darkness of this age, and against the spiritual forces of wickedness in the heavenly places. Therefore, put on the whole armor of God,* *that you may be able to withstand in the evil day, and having done all, to stand. Stand therefore, having the utility belt of truth buckled around your waist, and having put on the breastplate of righteousness, and having fitted your feet with the preparation of the Good News of peace, above all, taking up the shield of faith, with which you will be able to quench all the fiery darts of the evil one. And take the helmet of salvation, and the sword of the Spirit, which is the word of God; with all prayer and requests, praying at all times in the Spirit, and being watchful to this end in all perseverance and requests for all the saints.* WEB*

When we go back to bear fruit, we must first bind the strongman. According to Mark 3:27 *But no one can enter the house of the strong man to plunder, unless he first binds the strong man; and then he will plunder his house.* WEB

How can we do this if he fully guards his house according to Luke 11:21 *When the strong man, fully armed, guards his own dwelling, his goods are safe.* WEB

We must bind him and God has given us the power and authority through Christ Jesus. We have all of heaven backing us up according to Matthew 18:18 *Most certainly I tell you whatever things you bind on earth will have been bound in heaven, and whatever things you release on earth will have been released in heaven.* WEB

God gave us the binding and loosing power here on earth. This will allow His will to be done on earth through us and in earth which is in us. We are made from the dust of the earth and its elements are a part of us. His will be done on earth which is throughout the earth through us.

When we have been delivered and set free from what has us bound to the world and the flesh. We can loose meaning to let the Holy Spirit that is within us to use us and go bear the fruit God is calling for in these last and evil days.

CHAPTER 13

THE KINGDOM

In John 18:36 Jesus answered *My Kingdom is not of this world.*

We must be Kingdom mindset. 1 Corinthians 4:20 *For the Kingdom of God is not in word, but in power.* WEB

1 Corinthians 15:50 *Now I say this, brothers, that flesh and blood cannot inherit the Kingdom of God; neither does corruption inherit incorruption.* WEB

We must bring forth fruit in the Kingdom. Matthew 21:43 *Therefore I tell you; the Kingdom of God will be taken away from you, and will be given to a nation bringing forth its fruit.* WEB

2 Thessalonians 1:5 *This is an obvious sign of the righteous judgment of God, to the end that you may be counted worthy of the Kingdom of God, for which you also suffer.* WEB

The Kingdom of God and the Kingdom of heaven although may often be used interchangeably but they are not the same. We will briefly discuss the two in this chapter.

The Kingdom of God is right now and the Kingdom of heaven is in the future.

According to Matthew 6:33 We are to seek first God's Kingdom and His righteousness.

In Luke 17:20-21 Jesus says the kingdom of God does not come with observation and the Kingdom of God is in us.

Luke 10:9 says; Heal the sick in it and say to them, the Kingdom of God has come near you.

THE KINGDOM OF GOD IS RIGHTEOUSNESS AND PEACE AND JOY IN THE HOLY SPIRIT. (ROMAN 14:17) _{WEB}

As said in John 3:3 you MUST be born again to see this Kingdom. John 3:5 Jesus answered, "Most certainly I tell you, unless one is born of water and Spirit, we can't enter into the Kingdom of God!

In Acts 19:8 Jesus *entered into the synagogue and spoke boldly for a period of three months, reasoning and persuading about the things concerning God's Kingdom.* _{WEB}

Paul and Barnabas preached the gospel in a city and won a sizable number of disciples. Then they returned to other cities to appoint elders for them in each church. With prayer and fasting, wholeheartedly dedicated them to the Lord according to Acts 14:21 and 23. They had to build up the mind, will and emotions of the disciples urging them to carry on in faith because there would be many troubles they would have to face to enter God's Kingdom. This is found in Acts 14:22 *strengthening the souls of the disciples, exhorting them to continue in the faith, and that through many afflictions we must enter into God's Kingdom.*_{WEB}

We must also be committed to carry on in prayer and fasting in the faith building up and strengthening one another.

In Luke chapter seventeen verses twenty and twenty-one Jesus told the Pharisees that *The Kingdom of God does not come with observation; neither will they say, 'Look, here!' or, 'Look, there!' for behold, **the Kingdom of God is within you.*** _{WEB}

Matthew 23:14 *But woe to you, scribes and Pharisees, hypocrites! Because you shut up the Kingdom of Heaven against men; for you do not enter in yourselves, neither do you allow those who are entering in to enter.* _{WEB}

Ephesians 5:1-2 *Be therefore imitators of God, as beloved children. Walk in love, even as Christ also loved you, and gave himself up for us, an offering, and a sacrifice to God for a sweet-smelling fragrance.* _{WEB}

Ephesians 5:1-2 states that we are to follow God's example by walking in the way of love just as Christ did. This chapter and verses further tell us of the things we should not be doing or we will not inherit the Kingdom of Christ and of God ground in Ephesians 5:3-5. Scripture tells us in Ephesians 5:6-7 *Let no one deceive you with empty words. Because of these things, the wrath of God comes on the children of disobedience. Therefore, do not be partakers with them.* WEB

Let us take time to briefly look at a few parables on the Kingdom of God first in Luke 14:12-24 *He also said to the one who had invited Him, "When you make a dinner or a supper, don't call your friends, nor your brothers, nor your kinsmen* (relative), *nor rich neighbors, or perhaps they might also return the favor, and pay you back. But when you make a feast, ask the poor, the maimed, the lame, or the blind; and you will be blessed, because they do not have the resources to repay you. For you will be repaid in the resurrection of the righteous. When one of those who sat at the table with Him heard these things, He said to him, Blessed is he who will feast in God's Kingdom! But He said to him, "A certain man made a great supper, and He invited many people. He sent out His servant at supper time to tell those who were invited, Come, for everything is ready now. They all as one began to make excuses. The first said to Him, I have bought a field, and I must go and see it. Please have me excused. Another said, I have bought five yokes of oxen, and I must go try them out. Please have me excused. Another said, I have married a wife, and therefore I cannot come. That servant came, and told his Lord these things. Then the Master of the house, being angry, said to His servant, go out quickly into the streets and lanes of the city, and bring in the poor, maimed, blind, and lame. The servant said, Lord, it is done as you commanded, and there is still room. The Lord said to the servant, go out into the highways and hedges, and compel them to come in, that My house may be filled. For I tell you that none of those men who were invited will taste of my supper.* WEB

Revelation 19:7-9 *Let us rejoice and be exceedingly glad, and let us give the glory to Him. For the wedding of the Lamb has come, and his wife has made herself ready. It was given to her that she would array herself in bright, pure, fine linen: for the fine linen is the righteous acts of the saints. He said to me,*

*Write, blessed are those who are invited to the wedding supper of the Lamb.
He said to me, "These are true words of God."* _{WEB}

In Acts 8:12 *But when they believed Philip preaching good news concerning
God's Kingdom and the name of Jesus Christ, they were baptized, both men
and women.* _{WEB}

We are also informed not to let anyone deceive us with empty words
because the wrath of God comes on those who are disobedient. For us
not to even be partakers with them.

We must go back to the basic truth of when we first loved God. That
time where we first meet God. That moment we received Him and
became His children. When obstacles get in our way and we begin to
lose the joy of when we first received Christ. We must *pray that God will
restore the joy of our salvation back* (Psalm 51:12). The time when we could
barely quote a Scripture but we talked about our new found Joy. The
time when we did not think of ourselves more highly than we ought to.

When we were humble in knowing we needed Him.

When we just wanted everyone to know about Jesus and His goodness.
Just like the woman at the well when she dropped her water pots and
ran to tell them all to "come see about a man".

In Matthew 22:1-14 *of the World English Bible Jesus answered and spoke
to them again in parables, saying, The Kingdom of Heaven is like a certain
king, who made a wedding feast for his son, and sent out his servants to call
those who were invited to the wedding feast, but they would not come. Again,
he sent out other servants, saying, tell those who are invited, Behold, I have
prepared my dinner. My cattle and my fatlings are killed, and all things are
ready. Come to the wedding feast! But they made light of it, and went their
ways, one to his own farm, another to his merchandise; and the rest grabbed
his servants, treated them shamefully, and killed them. When the king heard
that, he was angry, and sent his armies, destroyed those murderers, and
burned their city. Then he said to his servants, the wedding is ready, but
those who were invited were not worthy. Go therefore to the intersections*

of the highways, and as many as you may find, invite to the wedding feast. Those servants went out into the highways and gathered together as many as they found, both bad and good. The wedding was filled with guests. But when the king came in to see the guests, he saw there a man who did not have on wedding clothing, and he said to him, 'Friend, how did you come in here not wearing wedding clothing? He was speechless. Then the king said to the servants, 'Bind him hand and foot, take him away, and throw him into the outer darkness. That is where the weeping and grinding of teeth will be. For many are called, but few chosen. _{WEB}*

"Repent, for the Kingdom of Heaven is at hand!"

Matthew 16:15-19 *He said to them, "But who do you say that I am?" Simon Peter answered, "You are the Christ, the Son of the living God." Jesus answered him, "Blessed are you, Simon Bar Jonah, for flesh and blood has not revealed this to you, but my Father who is in heaven. 18I also tell you that you are Peter, and on this rock, I will build my assembly, and the gates of Hades will not prevail against it. I will give to you the keys of the Kingdom of Heaven, and whatever you bind on earth will have been bound in heaven; and whatever you release on earth will have been released in heaven."* _{WEB}

Let us take time to briefly look at a few parables on the Kingdom of heaven. Jesus preached "Repent! For the Kingdom of Heaven is at hand." In Matthew 5:3 *Jesus said "Blessed are the poor in spirit, for theirs is the Kingdom of Heaven* and Matthew 5:10 *Blessed are those who have been persecuted for righteousness' sake, for theirs is the Kingdom of Heaven.* _{WEB}

Who is the least in the Kingdom of Heaven and why?

Who will be called great in the Kingdom of Heaven and why? Matthew 5:19-20 *Whoever, therefore, shall break one of these least commandments, and teach others to do so, shall be called least in the Kingdom of Heaven; but whoever shall do and teach them shall be called great in the Kingdom of Heaven. For I tell you that unless your righteousness exceeds that of the scribes and Pharisees, there is no way you will enter into the Kingdom of Heaven.* _{WEB}

Matthew 7:21 *Not everyone who says to Me, 'Lord, Lord,' will enter into the Kingdom of Heaven; but he who does the will of My Father who is in heaven.* WEB

Matthew 11:11-12 *Most certainly I tell you, among those who are born of women there has not arisen anyone greater than John the Baptizer; yet he who is least in the Kingdom of Heaven is greater than he. From the days of John, the Baptizer until now, the Kingdom of Heaven suffers violence, and the violent take it by force.* WEB

Jesus told His disciples to go preach the Kingdom of heaven is at hand. He also told them to make disciples in another verse. As His disciples we ought to do the same as He has taught in Matthew 10:7 *As you go, preach, saying, "The Kingdom of Heaven is at hand!"* WEB

There is a reason Jesus spoke in parables concerning the Kingdom, let us read in Matthew 13:10-15 *The disciples came, and said to Him, "Why do You speak to them in parables?" He answered them, "To you it is **given to know the mysteries of the Kingdom of Heaven**, but it is not given to them. For whoever has, to him will be given, and he will have abundance; but whoever does not have, from him will be taken away even that which he has. Therefore, I speak to them in parables, because seeing they do not see, and hearing, they do not hear, neither do they understand. In them the prophecy of Isaiah is fulfilled, which says, **by hearing you will hear, and will in no way understand; Seeing you will see, and will in no way perceive; for this people's heart has grown callous, their ears are dull of hearing, and they have closed their eyes; or else perhaps they might perceive with their eyes, hear with their ears, understand with their heart, and would turn again, and I would heal them. Isaiah 6:9-10.*** WEB

Matthew 13:24-30 He set another parable before them, saying, *The Kingdom of Heaven is like a man who sowed good seed in his field, but while people slept, his enemy came and sowed darnel weeds also among the wheat, and went away. But when the blade sprang up and produced grain, then the darnel weeds appeared also. The servants of the householder came and said to him, 'Sir, didn't you sow good seed in your field? Where did these darnel weeds* come from? He said to them, an enemy has done this. The servants asked him, "Do you want us to go and gather them up?" But he said, no, lest perhaps while you gather up the darnel weeds, you root up the wheat with them. Let both grow together until the harvest, and in the harvest time I will tell the reapers, "First, gather up the darnel weeds, and bind them in bundles to burn them; but gather the wheat into my barn. _{WEB}

Matthew 13:31-35 *He set another parable before them, saying, The Kingdom of Heaven is like a grain of mustard seed which a man took, and sowed in his field, which indeed is smaller than all seeds. But when it is grown, it is greater than the herbs and becomes a tree, so that the birds of the air come and lodge in its branches. He spoke another parable to them. The Kingdom of Heaven is like yeast which a woman took and hid in three measures of meal, until it was all leavened. Jesus spoke all these things in parables to the multitudes; and without a parable, he did not speak to them, that it might be fulfilled which was spoken through the prophet, saying.* _{WEB}

Psalm 78:2 *I will open my mouth in parables; I will utter things hidden from the foundation of the world.* _{WEB}

As we have reviewed many parables concerning the Kingdom of God and the Kingdom of Heaven here are a few more.

Matthew 13:44-45 *Again, the Kingdom of Heaven is like a treasure hidden in the field, which a man found, and hid. In his joy, he goes and sells all that he has, and buys that field. Again, the Kingdom of Heaven is like a man who is a merchant seeking fine pearls.* _{WEB}

Matthew 13:47 *Again, the Kingdom of Heaven is like a dragnet, that was cast into the sea, and gathered some fish of every kind.* _{WEB}

Matthew 13:52 *He said to them, "Therefore, every scribe who has been made a disciple in the Kingdom of Heaven is like a man who is a householder, who brings out of his treasure new and old things."* _{WEB}

Matthew 16:19 *I will give to you the keys of the Kingdom of Heaven, and whatever you bind on earth will have been bound in heaven; and whatever you release on earth will have been released in heaven.* WEB

Matthew 18:1-4 *In that hour the disciples came to Jesus, saying, "Who then is greatest in the Kingdom of Heaven?" and said, "Most certainly I tell you, unless you turn, and become as little children, you will in no way enter into the Kingdom of Heaven. Whoever therefore humbles himself as this little child, the same is the greatest in the Kingdom of Heaven.* WEB

Matthew 18:23 *Therefore the Kingdom of Heaven is like a certain king, who wanted to reconcile accounts with his servants.* WEB

Mathew 19:12 *For there are eunuchs who were born that way from their mother's womb, and there are eunuchs who were made eunuchs by men; and there are eunuchs who made themselves eunuchs for the Kingdom of Heaven's sake. He who is able to receive it, let him receive it.* WEB

Just as the Kingdom of Heaven belongs to the little children it also belongs to the adult children of God. Matthew 19:14 *But Jesus said, "Allow the little children, and don't forbid them to come to Me; for the Kingdom of Heaven belongs to ones like these.* WEB

It is hard to part a person with their money. Your treasure is where your heart is. The love of money is the root of all evil. Matthew 19:23 *Jesus said to His disciples, most certainly I say to you, a rich man will enter into the Kingdom of Heaven with difficulty.* WEB

Matthew 19:24 Again I tell you, it is easier for a camel to go through a needle's eye, than for a rich man to enter into the **Kingdom of God**. WEB

Mark 10:23-24 *Jesus looked around, and said to His disciples, how difficult it is for those who have riches to enter into the Kingdom of God! The disciples were amazed at His words. But Jesus answered again, Children, how hard is it for those who trust in riches to enter into the Kingdom of God!* WEB

We will briefly look at another kingdom that we do not want any part of. This will be a short message. He gets no glory. If you desire to know more about him or his kingdom, seek it through the Holy Scripture.

If we are in Christ and we obey His word. We love and do not hold any unforgiveness in our heart; the enemy cannot take advantage of us by Satan; for we will not be ignorant of his schemes. God will not leave us ignorant to any of his devices.

There is a kingdom of outer darkness where there will be weeping and gnashing of teeth according to Matthew chapter eight verse twelve.

Satan has a kingdom that is not divided. Contrary to widely held belief that God's Kingdom is divided. No! God's Kingdom that is not divided. According to Jesus in Matthew chapter twelve and verses twenty-five and twenty-six of the World English Bible *every kingdom divided against itself is brought to desolation, and every city or house divided against itself will not stand. If Satan casts out Satan, he is divided against himself. How then will his kingdom stand?*

1 Peter 5:8 *Be sober and self-controlled. Be watchful. Your adversary, the devil, walks around like a roaring lion, seeking whom he may devour.* WEB

We as believers have been delivered out of the power of darkness. Colossians 1:12-14 *giving thanks to the Father, who made us fit to be partakers of the inheritance of the saints in light; who delivered us out of the power of darkness, and translated us into the Kingdom of the Son of His love; in whom we have our redemption, the forgiveness of our sins.* WEB

The enemy will even use whoever allows him to use them. Until the Lord opens our eyes and spiritually a scale like substance falls off, we will not be able to see. The Lord sends people to open the blinded eyes of minds of the unbelievers. Once our eyes are open, He will also send us too when He is ready. So that others may turn from darkness the power of Satan to light the power of God.

We are told to share the gospel of Jesus, which is The Great Commission. Scripture mentioned after Jesus revealed Himself and rebuked the disciples for their unbelief and hardness of heart, because they did not believe those who had seen Him after He had risen. Then He said to them, *"Go into all the world, and preach the Good News to the whole creation. He who believes and is baptized will be saved; but he who disbelieves will be condemned. These signs will accompany those who believe: in my name they will cast out demons; they will speak with new languages; they will take up serpents; and if they drink any deadly thing, it will in no way hurt them; they will lay hands on the sick, and they will recover."* WEB God's desire is for none to perish. Jesus came to save those who are lost. That they may receive cancellation of sins and an inheritance to His Kingdom among those who are dedicated to God by faith in JESUS/YESHUA.

CHAPTER 14

TaGS aND TiTLeS

Take All Gifts Serious and
Trust In The Lord's Everlasting Spirit

This can be an obstacle in the way of many. All too often we go from title to title and instead from **faith to faith** found in Romans 1:17 and glory to glory found in 2 Corinthians 2:18.

When we have a gift and are too anxious to work in it, we will use the gifts as a title and not be able to properly function in that area; it becomes more of a name tag. Philippians 4:6 states *in nothing be anxious, but in everything, by prayer and petition with thanksgiving, let your requests be made known to God.* WEB

Now let us look at how important it is to do the work of an evangelist to make our ministry full proof according to 2 Timothy 4:5.

2 Timothy 4:1-5 *I command you therefore before God and the Lord Jesus Christ, who will judge the living and the dead at his appearing and his Kingdom:* **preach the word; be urgent in season and out of season; reprove, rebuke, and exhort, with all patience and teaching.** *For the time will come when they will not listen to the sound doctrine, but, having itching ears, will heap up for themselves teachers after their own lusts; and will turn away their ears from the truth, and turn aside to fables. But you be sober in all things, suffer hardship,* **do the work of an evangelist, and fulfill your ministry.** WEB

1 Timothy 4:14-16 **Don't neglect the gift that is in you,** *which was given to you by prophecy, with the laying on of the hands of the elders. Be diligent in these things. Give yourself wholly to them, that your progress may be revealed to all. Pay attention to yourself, and to your teaching. Continue in these things, for in doing this you will save both yourself and those who hear you.* WEB

Ephesians 4:11-14 *He gave some to be apostles; and some, prophets; and some, evangelists; and some, shepherds and teachers; for the perfecting of the saints, to the **work of serving**, to the building up of the body of Christ, **until we all attain to the unity of the faith and of the knowledge of the Son of God**, to a full grown man, to the measure of the stature of the fullness of Christ, that we may no longer be children, tossed back and forth and carried about with every wind of doctrine, by the trickery of men, in craftiness, after the wiles of error.* WEB·

If we see the five words from apostle to teacher in verse eleven. They are not written in capital letters as though they were titles. Therefore, they are not titles, they are gifts. In Ephesians 4:7-8 But to each one of us was the grace given according to the measure of the gift of Christ. Therefore, he says, ``When He ascended on high, He led captivity captive, and **gave gifts** to men." *WEB*

These are functions in the body, a work for serving until we all come into the full unity of Christ. Just because one is given the name apostle, prophet. evangelist, pastor, or teacher by another other than by God the name means little without the ability to function as one. Let us look a little bit deeper at the greetings from Paul in 1 Corinthians 1:1 "Paul, called to be an apostle of Jesus Christ through the will of God..." he did not say I AM APOSTLE PAUL.

An evangelist is not a title and evangelism is not an event but it is a work. In Proverbs 11:30 the one who wins souls is wise and they save lives. Matthew 10:16 *Behold, I send you out as sheep among wolves. Therefore, be wise as serpents and harmless as doves.* WEB

We must go back to the basics, to the time before the titles became name tags. The time before we got indoctrinated and caught up in organized religion. The time when we first received Jesus and was filled with His Holy Spirit. The time when we were running around telling everyone about Him and how He saved our soul. When we wanted everyone to experience this too. The time when we barely knew the Scriptures or the hermeneutics. When we did not know the name of the books in the

Bible or their order. All we knew is that it was in there and we could quote a piece of a verse. Then you would say, "I don't know where it is but it's in there." We might have even tried to look for it by flipping through the pages. Then we may even close the book and begin to testify with such love, joy, and zeal, of Jesus our new found treasure. The time before we may have gotten caught up in the title, the money, the sales, the service, theological training. Before you got the position or the office that you got caught up in the works and lost the real heart for what you were doing or neglected your true calling. In the book of Revelation it says return to your first love.

There are many others who refuse to go back to basics because of titles and prestige. There are ones who do not want to admit they are not in the area where God called them. There are others that allow others to keep them in a place or position that God did not give them. There are ones who have fallen and refuse to get back up due to guilt, shame, hurt and defeat. Letting the life trials beat up on you causing you to stay there all alone. Others have gotten caught up in the things of this world and its lust thereof. There are some who have been caught up in pride.

Go back to the time when you could not help yourself and you needed Jesus to be your Lord and Savior. The time when you Had faith in God, when you trusted Him, when you believed His Word. The time when we were nobody and no one did not even know our name. When we were trying to tell anyone and everybody who would listen, about Somebody by the name of Jesus. Like the woman at the well who dropped her water pots and ran back to tell them about a man who knew all she had done in John 4:28-29.

Now we are going to view this at another angle. There are ones who are doing the will of God in the Scripture. Even though the Spirit of God is using them they are being plotted on and lied on. There are many accounts throughout Scripture. We will take a glance at one account in Acts 6 of the World English Bible. We will view verses one through fifteen *Now in those days, when **the number of the disciples was multiplying, a complaint arose** from the Hellenists against the Hebrews, **because their widows were*** *neglected in the daily service. The twelve summoned the multitude of the disciples and said, "It is not appropriate for us to forsake the word of God and serve tables. Therefore, select from among you, brothers, seven men of good report, full of the Holy Spirit and of wisdom, whom we may appoint over this business. But we will continue steadfastly in prayer and in the ministry of the word." These words pleased the whole multitude. They chose Stephen, a man full of faith and of the Holy Spirit, Philip, Prochorus, Nicanor, Timon, Parmenas, and Nicolaus, a proselyte of Antioch; whom they set before the apostles. When **they had prayed, they laid their hands on them. The word of God increased and the number of the disciples greatly multiplied** in Jerusalem. A great company of the priests were obedient to the faith. Stephen, full of faith and power, performed great wonders and signs among the people. But some of those who were of the synagogue called "The Libertines," and of the Cyrenians, of the Alexandrians, and of those of Cilicia and Asia **arose, disputing with Stephen. They were not able to withstand the wisdom and the Spirit by which he spoke. Then they secretly induced men to say, "We have heard him speak blasphemous words against Moses and God." They stirred up the people, the elders, and the scribes, and came against him and seized him, then brought him in to the council, and set up false witnesses who said, "This man never stops speaking blasphemous words against this holy place and the law. For we have heard him say that this Jesus of Nazareth will destroy this place, and will change the customs which Moses delivered to us." All who sat in the council, fastening their eyes on him, saw his face like it was the face of an angel.***

The wicked will set up a false council against the people of God. Nevertheless we must set our faces as flint and continue in whatever gifts the Lord has given us. As a born-again believer you may not have a title but everyone has at least one or more spiritual gifts. It is important to find out what that gift is and serve. The best title we can have as children of God is being children. As children, we must serve Him. We are brothers and sisters therefore we ought to serve one another in love as unto the Lord.

1 Peter 3:15 *But **sanctify the Lord God in your hearts**. Always be ready to give an answer to everyone who asks you a reason concerning the hope that is in you, with humility and fear.* WEB

CHAPTER 15

THE NEXT GENERATION

Scripture tells us that the harvest is plentiful but the laborers are few (Matthew 9:35-38). God is waiting on His children and so is the next generation. We cannot just leave the next generation to figure things out for themselves. If they are left to process things for themselves, they will process it the only way they know how just like we did. Then the next generations get worse because of sin and lack of knowledge. Scripture tells us that knowledge will increase. We see this in worldly, scientific and technology knowledge.

When the knowledge of God is presented many reject it and even if they do not reject it the word is tugging on them. If we do not get rooted and grounded in the word of God and surround ourselves with the true church it can make the truth hard to receive. We are told to Study to show ourselves approved of God. Scripture also tells us bad company corrupts good morals.

It is our job as parents and guardians are to train up our children in the Lord as well as other things pertaining to life. That when they grow up, they will not depart from what they were taught. Even if they do leave, they will know how to return to the Father in heaven just like the Scripture on the prodigal son returning home to his father. That prodigal child will find himself or herself back in the loving arms of our Father in Heaven. Therefore, we have a job to do and that is to train the children in the love of the Lord. After all the children are our coming time and we must teach them well as they grow up to become leaders too. What better way than to train them for life with Jesus. Jesus is the answer and the cure we all need.

All converts must be trained in the Lord.

As Jesus' disciples we must learn to be disciplined. We must make and take time to study and learn of Him. We must meditate on His word, fast, pray and much more. We are not only to become converts but be converted to His ways to become more like Him. We must be born again of the water and the Spirit and the only way is through the Son of God. The Son of God is the Word of God and He can wash us and Give us His Spirit. Become one in the spirit and having no division amongst one another we are all equally and individually a part of God's body. Ephesians 6:1-4 ***Children, obey your parents in the Lord, for this is right. "Honor your father and mother," which is the first commandment with a promise:*** *"that it may be well with you, and you may live long on the earth." You fathers, do not provoke your children to wrath, but nurture them in the discipline and instruction of the Lord.* WEB

We too ought to become humble like one of these children know, listen, and obey the voice of God. Jesus said in Matthew 18:3 *and said, "Most certainly I tell you, unless you turn, and become as little children, you will in no way enter into the Kingdom of Heaven.* WEB

CHAPTER 16

PLAYTIME IS OVER

Armor up and put on the full armor of God playtime is over. Ephesians 6:10-17 *Finally, be strong in the Lord, and in the strength of his might.* Why must we put on the full armor of God? *Put on the whole armor of God,* ***that you may be able to stand against the wiles of the devil.*** *For our wrestling is not against flesh and blood,* our war is not with people ***but against the principalities, against the powers, against the world's rulers of the darkness of this age, and against the spiritual forces of wickedness in the heavenly places.*** *Therefore, put on the whole armor of God, that you may be able to withstand in the evil day, and, having done all, to stand. Stand therefore, having the utility belt of truth buckled around your waist, and having put on the breastplate of righteousness, and having fitted your feet with the preparation of the Good News of peace; all, taking up the shield of faith, with which you will be able to quench all the fiery darts of the evil one. And take the helmet of salvation, and the* ***sword of the Spirit, which is the word of God.*** WEB

Playtime is over for us whether we are together or not.

United we all stand and a kingdom divided by itself can and will not stand. We must love everyone but we must love God more. So, whoever decides to stay let them stay and whoever wants to leave sets themselves free and them free. That we may live in peace with man and God. We can reason together as children of the Most High but no longer compromise with the enemy or his disciples. There is a selected handful that we are in communication with. That handful is selected to communicate with us. They were either sent to us or we were led to them either by God or the enemy. We are to be in communication with our Father who is in heaven to order our footsteps. Relationships with one another are needed. We are not lone rangers Proverbs 27:17 *tells us that Iron sharpens Iron.* This is a positive statement that we can all use to become more effective in serving God and righteous living. *Faithful are the wounds of a friend, but deceitful are the kisses of an enemy* is found in Proverbs 27:6. _{WEB}

2 Timothy 3:16 Every *Scripture is God-breathed and profitable for teaching, for reproof, for correction, and for instruction in righteousness.* _{WEB}

Brothers and sisters take note of this: Everyone should be quick to listen to the Spirit of God, slow to speak what the Spirit of God says to say. We are slow to become angry.

Worldly anger produces unrighteousness but godly anger produces righteousness, Godly anger produces us to say what should be said through us by the Spirit of God. Just like when Jesus turned over the tables and said Matthew 21:13 *"It is written, 'My house shall be called a house of prayer, 'Isaiah 56:7 but you have made it a den of robbers! "Jeremiah 7:11.* _{WEB}

Hebrews 4:12 *For the word of God is living and active, and sharper than any two-edged sword, piercing even to the dividing of soul and spirit, of both joints and marrow, and is able to discern the thoughts and intentions of the heart according to.* _{WEB}

We are to build loving and growing relationships with our Father in heaven and with others. We need to be healed, delivered, and set free by the power of God through the precious blood of Jesus. We are to let nothing separate us from the love of God. We must be persuaded that neither death or life, nor angels, nor powers, nor things past, present, or future paraphrased from Romans 8:35-39. We must choose God but He gives us a free will choice and He will not make us choose Him. We cannot get caught up in the cares of this world. We must build our treasure in heaven. Friendship with the world is enmity with God, we are in the world but not of the world. We are a spiritual being in an earthly body that possesses a soul.

While we are on this earth in the body of Christ who is the true church is to seek the Kingdom of God for the Kingdom of Heaven is at hand.

The Kingdom of God does not come with observation but His kingdom is in the born-again believers and all around us. Let your Kingdom come. Matthew 6:10 *Let your will be done, as in heaven, so on earth.* _{WEB}

For His will to be done on earth it has to be done in earth and that is in us we were made from the earth.

The enemy also has a kingdom and has set it up and is setting it up for the last days. 2 Corinthians 11:4 *For if he who comes preaches another Jesus, whom we did not preach, or if you receive a different spirit, which you did not receive, or a different "good news", which you did not accept, you put up with that well enough. We cannot get around that it has been going on since the beginning of time but we have our part to do.* _{WEB}

News flash when the Antichrists finish setting up his kingdom. It will not matter if you are into spiritism, if you are an atheist, Muslim, Buddhist Christian, and anything else. Because he cares if you believe in him and worship him ONLY. He wants all to worship and receive the mark HIS MARK. Therefore, make your election very sure. He wants our faith because without faith it is impossible to please our Father in Heaven. When Jesus returns, He wants to find faith in the earth. CHOOSE YOU THIS DAY WHICH GOD YOU WILL SERVE... The time is now ready for His return. Don't you want to hear Jesus/ Yeshua say well done my good and faithful servant? Jesus is the name above every name. The name by which humankind can be saved. The name demons tremble and flee. That name whereby every knee will bow and every tongue will confess that he is Lord. They may not bow now but they will bow in the end for God's word is true. That precious name is Jesus the Christ. AT THAT NAME JESUS THE CHRIST. HIS NAME IS SO POWERFUL THE PEOPLE OF GOD LOVE HIM. SO POWERFUL DEMONS AND OTHERS HATE JESUS AND HIS TRUE FOLLOWERS. Luke 21:17-19 You *will be hated by all men for my name's sake. And not a hair of your head will perish. "By your endurance you will win your lives.* _{WEB}

CHAPTER 17

OPEN DOORS

There are many open doors the enemy uses but the one open door that he does not need permission. That door is through music, it is a legal entry. Music is the open door that the ENEMY do not need permission to access you or your children. What are you feeding your spirit? Entertainment is not just entertainment... We have gateways to the soul as a reminder our soul is our mind, will and emotions. It is through our EYES/SIGHT we fulfill the lust of the eyes; we are told to walk by faith and not by sight. It is through our EARS we receive SOUND and is where our faith is tested because faith comes by, HEARING. We must silence all others' voices except the Voice of God and the Word of God. It is in our MOUTH we have TASTE we are told to taste and see that the Lord is good. We must have an appetite for Him. Our NOSE, SMELL, TOUCH, EVEN SEX play a role in the lust of our flesh, these are gateways used by the enemy to get us to sin.

WE ARE SPIRIT, BODY AND SOUL... We are spiritual beings housed in a body that has a soul (mind, will and emotions). We are made of the earth's elements dirt, water and so on. The body will one day return to that but the spirit returned to where it came according to the word of God. Our body is made up of over 70 percent of water. It was said to me at an early age when people start acting wild the older folks would say; "is it a full moon." Many times, when there is a full moon the water in the oceans rises and people will begin to act out due to the levels within them rises. All I know is according to Scripture, no flesh and blood will be able to enter the Kingdom of Heaven, we will be changed. No flesh and blood can enter that Kingdom... We are made of the earth and its elements; we are so closely related to the earth we are in constant war between the flesh and the spirit. It is a war within... Whichever one we are ruled by, that is what we are controlled by. If we are ruled by our flesh our soul gravitates towards fleshly desires of the world and worldly things. If we are led or ruled by the Spirit then our soul is gravitated to spiritual things of the spirit and is ruled by it. The ENEMY uses the Lust of the eyes, the lust of the flesh and the pride of life. He tempts all of us with those three things... But not all of us desire or are tempted by the same temptations... Be on your guard the adversary comes seeking whom he may devour... Jesus has come to destroy the works of the devil... He will not have us ignorant to the enemy's devices.

CHAPTER 18

THE OFFENDED

We must learn to love DESPITE of everything the offence will come. We may offend someone or someone may offend us.

Note: When you have warned people by the Spirit of God and the Word of God. Some may listen and take heed to what the Lord has said through you, they will repent and turn to God. Or God may have given someone a word for us and we may receive and repent. Yet! Others may get upset with you and do not want to hear or listen to what God has said through the individual. It can be any number of reasons that the person will not receive the message. When God has said it to the person, they must be obedient. Once we have done what God told us to do then the blood is off your hands. If they refuse to listen or obey, that is no longer on you. They did not reject you; they rejected God and God alone. You did not reject them, you rejected God and only God. Because what was said and done opened the door to being offended through either hurt or rejection. Now! You are offended and walking in the spirit of offense and the "inner me" which is the inner you agree with the enemy. You will be walking in err offended at your brother or sister when it is really God that you are unknowingly offended at. You have done your part NOW Shake the dust off your feet. Let your peace return to you. MOVE on to the next assignment the Lord has given you. Now let them choose their own path. Stop casting your pearls on non-receptive people.

You must learn to be careful and prayerful on what you say when others come to you venting concerning others. They will take your responses to heart or when they are done venting they will reveal what you said in a negative way.

Even be prayerful when others come back to you out of the blues, disappear, reappear and so on. They will disappear and reappear for two reasons: to check on the negative or the positive things in your life. Either way they do not want you to succeed so do not be so eager to allow the offended back into your life but we must forgive. Luke 17:3 Tells us to *be careful. If your brother sins against you, rebuke him. If he repents, forgive him.* Also, according to Matthew 16:5 *But if you do not forgive men their trespasses, neither will your Father forgive your trespasses.* WEB

Matthew 5:22-25 *But I tell you, that everyone who is angry with his brother without a cause shall be in danger of the judgment; and whoever shall say to his brother, 'Raca!' shall be in danger of the council; and whoever shall say, 'You fool!' shall be in danger of the fire of Gehenna. "If therefore you are offering your gift at the altar, and there remember that your brother* or sister *has anything against you, leave your gift there before the altar, and go your way. First be reconciled to your brother* or sister, *and then come and offer your gift. Agree with your adversary quickly.* WEB

Matthew 18:15-20 *If your brother* or sister *sins against you, go, show him his fault between you and him* or her *alone. If he* or she *listens to you, you have gained back your brother* or sister. *But if he* or she *does not listen, take one or two more with you, that at the mouth of two or three witnesses every word may be established. If he* or she *refuses to listen to them, tell it to the assembly. If he* or she *refuses to hear the assembly also, let him* or her *be to you as a Gentile or a tax collector. Most certainly I tell you, whatever things you bind on earth will have been bound in heaven, and whatever things you release on earth will have been released in heaven. Again, assuredly I tell you, that **if two of you will agree on earth concerning anything that they will ask, it will be done for them by my Father who is in heaven. For where two or three are gathered together in my name, there I am in the midst of them.*** WEB

CHAPTER 19

YOU WILL KNOW THEM

We must even recognize when a new person comes into your life; They were sent either by God or the enemy. Watch as well as pray because their words will not line up with their actions. By the time you realize what is going on many times your heart is already in it.

Scripture tells us to guard our hearts with all diligence and also tells us to put a guard on our mouth. We are slow to speak and quick to listen. We must hear, listen, and obey what the Spirit of God is saying to us as well as what is coming from the person speaking. We must realize who is speaking. With the gifts of God, we will be able to discern. When we know that it is God's Spirit speaking, we must silence the other voices through our obedience. We must not grieve the Holy Spirit who is sealed in every born-again believer until the day Jesus returns. He is sealed to lead, guide, comfort, protect us, bring to our remembrance everything Jesus taught and more. He will unction us when to speak and when to be silent. He will tell us when and where to go or not to go.

The enemy will send people to you in private and wear you out. You can labor in the spirit with them and then they will publicly thank someone else. They may even act like they are for you, in your face and be sabotaging you at the same time. Sometimes others may even try to warn you about them but you do not take heed. You will not receive what they said about them because you do not see it or your love for them is strong. You may have been deeply hurt by the betrayal of a friend or a loved one. Do not let this worry or bother you another day. Scripture says we will know them by their fruits. Yet we missed the red flags and or the warning signs. Give God all the glory, honor, praise, worship, and thanks that is due to Him. He will not leave us ignorant to Satan's devices. It did not kill you and you did not die during it so that means there is a purpose for you and God wants to heal, deliver, and set you free. God will get the glory out of our lives once that is done. Nothing of our self or by human means but God so that no human should get the glory, honor, praise, and worship that belongs to our Father in heaven. Even when we help one another to God be all the Glory BECAUSE NEITHER ONE Of US DID IT for without God, we can do nothing. We only can be used by God to water and/or plant but IT WAS GOD WHO GAVE THE INCREASE in the lives of His people. God uses human participant according to Luke 6:38. As the salt of the earth we were strategically shaken all over the earth like salt shaken out of a shaker. Matthew 5:13 tells us we are the salt of the earth. We must be available; we also have to an able and willing vessel to be used by the Lord. To serve Him though our obedience to Him.

And trust that the Lord will make a way because He is the way. Without faith it is very impossible to please God. First, we must believe that He is and once we believe the blinders will come off the eyes of our mind. He is a rewarder to all who diligently seek Him. We must seek first His Kingdom and all His righteousness. Then He will add natural and spiritual things unto us.

According to 1 Peter 4:10 God gives us gifts in the body of Christ. These gifts are ministry gifts found in Ephesians 4:11, manifestation gifts found in 1 Corinthians 12:7-10 and motivational gifts found in Romans 12:6-8. Romans 12:1-5 *Therefore I urge you, brothers, by the mercies of God, to present your bodies a living sacrifice, holy, acceptable to God, which is your spiritual service.*

Do not be conformed to this world, but be transformed by the renewing of your mind, so that you may prove what is the good, well-pleasing, and perfect will of God. For I say through the grace that was given me, to every man who is among you, not to think of himself more highly than he ought to think; but to think reasonably, as God has apportioned to each person a measure of faith. For even as we have many members in one body, and all the members do not have the same function, so we, who are many, are one body in Christ, and individually members of one another. WEB

CHAPTER 20

FORGIVENESS

We cannot keep doing things the world's way and call it God or expect God's results. When we are tempted Scripture tells us He makes a way of escape. 1 Corinthians 10:13 *No temptation has taken you except what is common to man. God is faithful, who will not allow you to be tempted above what you are able, but will with the temptation also make the way of escape, that you may be able to endure it.* _{WEB}

God does have an order contrary to popular beliefs that we can do things our own way. We cannot do what is right in our own eyes according to Proverbs 14:12 *There is a way which seems right to a man, but in the end, it leads to death.* _{WEB}

We must not hold on to guilt but be convicted enough to repent. 1 John 1: 8-10 *If we say that we have no sin, we deceive ourselves, and the truth is not in us. If we confess our sins, he is faithful and righteous to forgive us the sins, and to cleanse us from all unrighteousness. If we say that we have not sinned, we make him a liar, and his word is not in us.* _{WEB}

We must not hold on to being stuck in unforgiveness. There is a verse in the book of Matthew that tells us why its vitally important to forgive let us view Matthew 6:15 *But if you do not forgive men their trespasses, neither will your Father forgive your trespasses.* _{WEB}

How does forgiveness help us move on? When we forgive one another, others and forgive ourselves? It keeps that person, place, or thing from holding us hostage. It also keeps us from holding it or them hostage in our mind, heart, soul, and spirit. We can conquer that thing that tried to conquer us. According to Romans 8:37 *we are more than conquerors through Him who loved us.* They have moved on and are long gone so we must free them to free ourselves in order truly and freely move on. Holding on to unforgiveness causes all kinds of sickness, illnesses and issues in our life and body, Forgiveness is not for them it is for us, Forgiveness does not excuse them of what they did but it frees you. If they want forgiveness, they also must go to God the same way we did. Many times we must go back to the person or they must come back to us and seek forgiveness. However, we must learn to forgive even without an apology. Even on the cross Jesus said father forgive them they know not what they do even as they casted lots for His garment in Luke 23:34-35

Now forgiveness does not necessarily mean allowing them back in your life no more than it means never letting them back in your life. That is a decision between you and God. Majority of the time a space for an apology is not there. It could be because the person may be unreachable due to many different circumstances. Sometime they have passed away, are unable to find or just will not be a wise decision because it is too dangerous but nevertheless we have God to go to and seek His forgiveness just do not allow some kind of deception like pride, guilt, shame, hate or something holding you back for asking or receiving it concerning others. 2 Corinthians 2:7-11 *so that on the contrary you should rather forgive him* or her *and comfort him* or her*, lest by any means such a one should be swallowed up with his* or her *excessive sorrow. Therefore, I beg you to confirm your love toward him* or her*. For to this end I also wrote, that I might know the proof of you, whether you are obedient in all things. Now I also forgive whomever you forgive anything. For if indeed I have forgiven anything, I have forgiven that one for your sakes in the presence of Christ,* ***that no advantage may be gained over us by Satan, for we are not ignorant of his schemes.*** _{WEB}

CHAPTER 21

UNGODLY ADVICE

Let us look at a few chapters in the book of Psalms of the first chapter. *Psalm 1:1 Blessed is the man* (woman or child) *who does not walk in the counsel of the wicked, nor stand on the path of sinners, nor sit in the seat of scoffers;* WATCH WHERE YOU STAND, WALK AND SIT. *2 but his delight is in Yahweh's law. On his law he meditates day and night.* Hiding God's word in our heart that we do not sin against God is Meditating on God's word. We are to meditate so that we may be careful to do all that is written in it and by doing that then we will make our way prosperous, and have success. Psalm 1:3-6 *He will be like a tree planted by the streams of water, that produces its fruit in its season, whose leaf also does not wither. Whatever he does shall prosper. The wicked are not so, but are like the chaff which the wind drives away. Therefore, the wicked shall not stand in the judgment, nor sinners in the congregation of the righteous. For Yahweh knows the way of the righteous, but the way of the wicked shall perish.* WEB

Taking ungodly advice is taking advice from anyone and I mean anyone whose words are not based on or backed by Scripture. IT DOESN'T MATTER WHO THEY ARE. If their council is not from the Spirit of God. It is from the human spirit (fleshly and worldly) or from the ENEMY.

Listen: Galatians 6:1 *Brothers (*and sisters), *even if a man (*Or woman) *is caught in some fault, you who are spiritual must restore such a one in a spirit of gentleness; looking to yourself so that you also are not tempted.* WEB

When someone acknowledges the truth concerning the sin they are in and says, "if I go to hell I go to hell or if I die, I die." Proverb 18:31 The tongue can bring death or life; those who love to talk will reap the consequences. They have already chosen which god they will serve, notice it is a little "g". According Joshua "If serving the LORD seems undesirable to you, then choose for yourselves this day whom you will serve."

There is nothing you can do for them but pray. Their mind is made up for that moment "there is a pleasure in sin for a season" or forever sin breeds sin then death (spiritual then natural). They must be transformed by the renewing of their mind.

If one continues giving what is holy or casting your pearls, they may trample you under their feet, and turn and tear you to pieces.

Shake the dust from your feet and let your peace return to you. Live in peace with all humankind.

We cannot keep going in circles talking and beating people over the head with the Bible Scripture. No more than we can sugar coat or water down the word of God.

God is showing His grace and mercy toward us. He is giving us a chance to return to Him individually and collectively. We all must come into true repentance to God.

CHAPTER 22

DO IT AS UNTO THE LORD

Whatever it is that you are doing, make sure you are doing it as unto the Lord. Whether it is giving or sowing or anything in-between. We are God's lenders according to Scripture found in Proverb 19:17 *He who has pity on the poor* **lends to Yahweh; He will reward him**. WEB

God has our reward not humankind in Matthew 6:3-4 *But when you give to the poor, do not let your left hand know what your right hand is doing, so that your giving will be in secret; and your* **Father who sees what is done in secret will reward you**. WEB

You can do a million things for someone and they will not acknowledge what has been done or what you have done. But another person can come and do one thing, even say one word or do what you've been doing all along and the praises are never ending. Do not worry or get upset God sees all that you do and have done. Just remain humble remembering we reap what we sow but not necessarily where we sow it.

Matthew 6:20 *But store up for yourselves treasures in heaven, where neither moth nor rust destroys, and where thieves do not break in or steal.* WEB

Do not begin to talk about what you have done for others. In Matthew 6:1-4 *Be careful that you do not do your charitable giving before men, to be seen by them, or else you have no reward from your Father who is in heaven. Therefore, when you do merciful deeds, do not sound a trumpet before yourself, as the hypocrites do in the synagogues and in the streets, that they may get glory from men. Most certainly I tell you, they have received their reward. But when you do merciful deeds, do not let your left hand know what your right hand does, so that your merciful deeds may be in secret, then your Father who sees in secret will reward you openly.* WEB

Do not throw what you have done for someone up in their face. Do not run to others talking about them and what you have done for them. Do not even begin to regret doing it for them. If they want to tell others what you have done for them that is fine according to Proverb 21:2 tells us to *Let another man praise you, and not your own mouth; a stranger, and not your own lips.* WEB

God will supply all or your needs and He will repay you.

David said in Psalm 37:25-26 *I have been young and now I am old, Yet I have not seen the righteous forsaken or his descendants begging bread. All day long he is gracious and lends, and his descendants are a blessing.* WEB

According to Luke 6:8 we are to pray for those who mistreat or use you. When we pray God will help us and reveal to us what to do and show us who is who. Only what we do for Christ counts not your dollars and the amounts. Colossians 3:23 *And whatever you do, work heartily, as for the Lord, and not for men.* WEB

CHAPTER 23

WHO iS iN MY Life?

In 1 John 4:1 of the World English Bible testing the spirits and DO NOT *believe every spirit, but test the spirits, whether they are of God.*

Not everyone comes with a bad motive. But no matter who comes they were sent. It is extremely important to know who sent them. It is just as important to know who is in our life and why. When too often it is hard to know others but Scripture says we will know them by their fruits.

We must pay attention to the sign. Many times, we misread or read too much into it based on our own experiences, issues, fears and/or traumas. Often, we let others in our life who may only have been a brief encounter. Yet other times we may have gotten rid of someone who should have been there until the assignment is over. Even such people can be lifers or long term.

Sometimes when people stay in your life longer than they are supposed to, then the ending ends ugly. This does not always mean that either of the parties are bad. It may mean we need to work on ourselves. It could mean it is time to give the person time to work on themselves. It could mean one or both of you need a brief break to learn to appreciate what you have. It could just mean that it is time for new beginnings. Out with the old & in with the new do not mean that the love must be through. It is just that you put the love in a different place and space. Some people are lifers and some people are passersby and others are in your life for a season.

CHAPTER 24

DO NOT TAKE FOR GRANTED

We must not take anyone for granted. The tables can turn quick. Proverbs 6:16-19 *There are six things which Yahweh hates; yes, seven which are an abomination to him: arrogant eyes, a lying tongue, hands that shed innocent blood, a heart that devises wicked schemes, feet that are swift in running to mischief, a false witness who utters lies, and he who sows discord among brothers.* WEB

Just because someone wants you in their life does not mean they need you. Just because someone needs you in their life does not mean they want you in it. God hates a liar and according to Revelation 31:8 *liars, their part is in the lake that burns with fire and sulfur, which is the second death.* WEB

Do not take advantage of anyone nor take others for granted. Just recognize the difference and do your part. Decide when to hold on or when to let go. Because you can push your very blessing away or hold on to what is hindering you.

Many hold on to people for varied reasons such as financial. They may not want to be alone. They may share material things that they do not want to give up. It could be that the passion is great. It could be because the person is reliable, dependable, or available, the list goes on. We cannot just hold on to some with the wrong motives if our heart is not in it. *God hates a heart that devises wicked schemes.* Neither are we to hold on if God is not in it. People who have less to nothing will share everything. Many times, people fall in love with what the person does for them long before they fall in love with the person. Other times you can love a person long before they have done anything for you. When you can love a person unconditionally, that is where the favor of God rests on. The person may not have what you want or need but God supplies all the needs.

Most people with abundance are willing to share little to none of what they have. As we look at this principle in 1 Corinthians 9:6 Remember that they who sows sparingly will also reap sparingly. That is why money seems to slip through your fingers or when you get it something causes you to have to spend it. The world tells you to hold on to what you have or grab what you can. The Word of God says give in Luke 6:38 *Give, and it will be given to you: good measure, pressed down, shaken together, and running over, will be given to you. For with the same measure, you measure it will be measured back to you.* WEB

Do not take for granted when others do for you because God uses human participants. Be grateful for what seems like the smallest thing. We are not to take our parents for granted. We are not to take our spouse for granted. We are not to take our children for granted. Give God all the glory, honor, and praise. Most importantly do not take our heavenly Father for granted in Psalm 103:1-21 *Praise Yahweh, my soul! All that is within me, praise His Holy name! Praise Yahweh, my soul, and do not forget all His benefits; Who forgives all your sins; Who heals all your diseases; Who redeems your life from destruction; Who crowns you with lovingkindness and tender mercies; Who satisfies your desire with good things, so that your youth is renewed like the eagle's. Yahweh executes righteous acts, and justice for all who are oppressed. He made known His ways to Moses, His deeds to the children of Israel. Yahweh is merciful and gracious, Slow to anger, and abundant in lovingkindness. He will not always accuse; Neither will he stay angry forever. He has not dealt with us according to our sins, nor rewarded us for our iniquities. For as the heavens are high above the earth, so great is His loving kindness toward those who fear Him. As far as the east is from the west, so far has He removed our transgressions from us. Like a father has compassion on his children, So Yahweh has compassion on those who fear Him. For He knows how we are made. He remembers that we are dust. As for man, his days are like grass. As a flower of the field, so he flourishes. For the wind passes over it, and it is gone. Its place remembers it no more. But Yahweh's lovingkindness is from everlasting to everlasting with those who fear Him,*

His righteousness to children's children; To those who keep His covenant, to those who remember to obey His precepts. Yahweh has established His throne in the heavens. His kingdom rules over all. Praise Yahweh, you angels of His, who are mighty in strength, who fulfill His word, Obeying the voice of His Word. Praise Yahweh, all you host of His, you servants of His, who do His pleasure. Praise Yahweh, all you work of His, In all places of His dominion. Praise Yahweh, my soul. WEB

CHAPTER 25

THE MISSING VOID

Many times, too often someone will try to fill that missing void. They will fill it with alcohol, drugs, a person, a job etc. Whatever the nouns (people, places, or things) are in our lives we will use those as fillers. Many use that word I love you so loosely until they can say it with a straight face. They can say it with fake, no, or little emotions attached to it. One can say I love you and really think they mean it just because they had an intimate relationship with someone. That is not love, that is lust one may have gotten caught up in the moment. There is pleasure in sin for a season but when that season is over then it is over.

Just because someone tells you they love you does not mean they do. Just because they do not tell you they love you does not mean they do not. 1 Corinthians 13:4-7 *Love is patient and is kind; love does not envy. Love does not brag, is not proud, does not behave itself inappropriately, does not seek its own way, is not provoked, takes no account of evil; does not rejoice in unrighteousness, but rejoices with the truth; bears all things, believes all things, hopes all things, endures all things.* WEB

When God is not the filler of that missing void in our life, we tend to fill it with other fillers. Those fillers are the nouns in our lives. Those fillers can be sex, drugs, alcohol, gambling you name it. God reserves that space for Just for Him and Him alone. Nothing can fill that void but Him.

JESUS is knocking on your door. Will you let Him in?

God is calling you. Will you answer the call?

SOMEONE needs a spiritual awakening Yeshua says: "Our friend Lazarus is asleep, but I am going to awaken him." Yeshua is the resurrection and the life. Not just in this life but the life to come. 1 Corinthians 13:45-49 *So also it is written, "The first man, Adam, became a living soul." The last Adam became a life-giving spirit. However, that which is spiritual is not first, but that which is natural, then that which is spiritual. The first man is of the earth, made of dust. The second man is the Lord from heaven. As is the one made of dust, such are those who are also made of dust; and as is the heavenly, such are they also that are heavenly. As we have borne the image of those made of dust, let us also bear the image of the heavenly.* WEB

If we keep our minds on God, He will keep us in perfect peace no matter what is going on around us. Romans 8:5 *For those who live according to the flesh set their minds on the things of the flesh, but those who live according to the Spirit, the things of the Spirit.* WEB

God wants to free some people from the bad decisions they made without Him and called it God. He wants to free us from sin. He wants to free us from Satan's lies. John 8:36 says *If therefore the Son makes you free, you will be free indeed.* WEB

The missing void in your life is reserved for God. He is the only One who can FILL IT. Throughout the Old and the New Testaments God said He is Jealous. I will share part of this Scripture with you in 1 Corinthians 11:2 *For I am jealous over you with a godly jealousy.* WEB

We can search all over and not a man, not a woman, not a child, not our parents, not a job, not a car, not a house, not clothes, not shoes, not our spiritual or natural leaders, not money, not drugs, not alcohol, not sex, not sports, not politics, not birthdays or holidays, not a title or a name tag, not a degree, not a sugar daddy/momma, not the club, not friends, not family, not social media, not being famous, not being rich, etc. Nothing will be able to fill the void in our life, because when it is all said and done, we will still have a void without God BECAUSE ALL those things are a temporary fix. Amen

CHAPTER 26

POWER SOURCE

Zechariah 4:6 *Not by might, nor by power, but by My Spirit,' says Yahweh.* WEB

Many believers from the pulpit to the door are experiencing death like symptoms because they refuse to follow what Scriptures say. We cannot operate in our own might or power; we must operate by the Spirit of God.

DON'T ALWAYS feel wrong about EVERYTHING. God does not operate in our feelings but He operates in Spirit and in Truth according to His will. We must trust God, have faith, do not be afraid, believe. Do not allow everyone to KEEP blaming you for every dreadful thing that happens. REMEMBER A BROKEN CLOCK IS RIGHT TWICE A DAY. Remember shift blame is in the Scripture starting with Adam in Genesis 3:12 of the World English Bible *The man said, "The woman whom you gave to be with me, she gave me of the tree, and I ate."* and in verse thirteen *Yahweh God said to the woman, "What is this you have done?" The woman said, "The serpent deceived me, and I ate."* Therefore the shift blame is incredibly old.

We must take responsibility for our own actions. No matter how many times we shift the blame the consequences will fall on the person doing the shifting. You just may have to use a different outlet or plug. And plug into a different group of people, get another source of power/energy (our Heavenly Father is the best Source & the Highest Power) or you just charge or need to change your battery that may be the spiritually dead hindrance.

You never know what you have if you keep being around the same people and not allowing others to come into your life. Spiritual growth is necessary, not everyone has bad motives. When they are available, able, and willing to use their gifts to help others.

When they are not given opportunity or little opportunity to be used in a particular area. When someone else recognizes the help, gift, or talent in what you have been missing. The gifts will make room for the person, the blessings of the Lord make us rich and add no sorrow, and the blessings will chase us down and overtake us.

When a person is not spiritual they do not recognize their gifts. One may recognize their gifts but refuse to use them. The gifts & talents trapped inside are waiting to be used. For many reasons, the world gets so many gifted and talented people from the body of believers.

There are many leaders in the body of Christ who have experienced burnout. The members are burning out from no help and for that reason they keep using the same people repeatedly. In 2 Thessalonians tell us not to be weary in doing well. Many are getting frustrated and keep trying to do it themselves. Some are getting weary and Scripture tells us in Galatians 6:9 *Let us not be weary in doing good, for we will reap in due season, if we do not give up.* WEB

When we are told in Scripture that our GIFTS WILL MAKE ROOM FOR US. DON'T CLOSE THE DOOR AND IF THE DOOR IS CLOSED ANOTHER ONE WILL OPEN. DON'T WALK THROUGH EVERY OPEN DOOR. SOMETIMES THE WRONG DOOR WILL BE OPENED BY THE ENEMY. WAIT ON THE LORD AND BE OF GOOD COURAGE. YOUR BLESSINGS WILL CHASE YOU DOWN AND OVERTAKE YOU.

Always aim to please God and not people because no matter what you do there will always be people who will never be satisfied.

CHAPTER 27

WANT VS. NEED

Paraphrasing Ecclesiastes 10:19 *says that money is the answer for all things.* Every time I hear someone say that quote, I am convinced that that is not the intent of the message. I believe YES! For all worldly things but not spiritual things.

1 Timothy 6:10 *For the love of money is a root of all kinds of evil. Some have been led astray from the faith in their greed, and have pierced themselves through with many sorrows.* WEB

People young and old make foolish sacrifices over what they want versus what they need. Then EXPECT someone to meet their wants and needs or God to perform a miracle. God meets our needs and He will always meet our needs. Philippians 4:19 *My God will supply every need of yours according to His riches in glory in Christ Jesus.* WEB

It is one thing not to be able to meet your own needs. It is another to have provision to meet the need and you blow it on other stuff. And I am not talking about robbing Peter to pay Paul. It is our own habits and doing something that God did not tell us to do with it. God wants us to be good stewards over what He blesses us with.

He does not want us to love money or the things here on this earth but to be content with what we have because He is there with us. Hebrews 13:5 *Be free from the love of money, content with such things as you have, for he has said, "I will in no way leave you, neither will I in any way forsake you.* WEB

1 John 2:15 *Do not love the world or the things that are in the world. If anyone loves the world, the Father's love is not in him.* WEB

He wants us to sow on good ground. Here in Mark Jesus tells us a parable of a farmer and a sower. He is talking about the word of God but this is the same principle in chapter four verse twenty *Those which were sown on the good ground are those who hear the word, and accept it, and bear fruit, some thirty times, some sixty times, and some one hundred times.* WEB

To do that we have to ask Him and let Him speak. Then we must be willing to obey His voice and no other voice. John 10:27-30 *My sheep hear My voice, and I know them, and they follow Me. I give eternal life to them. They will never perish, and no one will snatch them out of My hand. My Father, who has given them to Me, is greater than all. No one is able to snatch them out of My Father's hand. I and the Father are one.* WEB

Whenever we give Luke 6:38 *Give, and it will be given to you: good measure, pressed down, shaken together, and running over, will be given to you. For with the same measure, you measure it will be measured back to you.* WEB

GIVE GOD WHAT HE WANTS AND HE WILL GIVE YOU WHAT YOU NEED 2 Corinthians 9:6 *Remember this: he who sows sparingly will also reap sparingly. He who sows bountifully will also reap bountifully. 7 Let each man* or woman *give according as he* or she *has determined in his* or her *heart; not grudgingly, or under compulsion; for God loves a cheerful giver. 8 And God is able to make all grace abound to you, that you, always having all sufficiency in everything, may abound to every excellent work.* WEB

HE WILL TELL YOU WHEN, WHERE, HOW, WHAT TO DO WITH WHAT HE HAS BLESSED YOU WITH. DO NOT BE CONTROLLED, MANIPULATED, INTIMIDATED, COHORTS TO DO What others want you to do or what you want to do. Be led by the Spirit of God IT'S A HEARTS CONDITION AND IT'S BETWEEN YOU AND GOD.

CHAPTER 28

POWeR aND aUTHORiTY

God has given His children power and authority to speak over our own sicknesses, issues, and situations... Okay! There may be a certain sickness, symptoms, diagnosis in manifestation. We are to speak those things that are not as though they were according to Romans 4:17 *There is the power of death and life that lies in our own tongue.* Our faith in God to do exceedingly and abundantly all that we may ask or think... Knowing that we can ask in the name of Jesus. Believing He is a rewarder to them who diligently seek Him. Believe in our heart and minds through faith in Him, not doubting or being afraid. You may feel the evidence of the pain but Scripture tells us to think on certain thoughts. Our thoughts effect and affect us more than we know. So, a person thinks so are they (Proverbs 23:7). Therefore, if you think sick then...and the same as if you think healed... For example, when a pain hits a certain area and IT'S TRYING TO CLAIM THAT AREA OR CLAIM YOU. Now you say I have a pain in so and so or MY so and so hurt. NOW YOU JUST CAME IN AGREEMENT WITH THAT PAIN AND CONNECTED IT WITH YOUR SO AND SO. THE POWER OF AGREEMENT.... FOR EXAMPLE, WE CAN SAY THIS PAIN IN MY XYZ. OR THE PAIN OR SICKNESS HAS MANIFESTED XYZ BUT IT HAS TO GO IN THE NAME OF JESUS... OR I BIND THIS OR THAT... OR PAIN LOOSE UR HOLD. PAIN OBEY THE SPIRIT OF THE LIVING GOD...YOU MAY EVEN HAVE TO LAY YOUR HANDS ON THE AREA...

Another example is when the doctor gives you a report. You can word it as such the doctor(s) said I have so and so but SCRIPTURE SAYS BY HIS STRIPES I AM HEALED. I BELIEVE THE REPORT OF THE LORD, NO WEAPONS FORMED AGAINST ME SHALL BE ABLE TO PROSPER AND/ OR ANY SCRIPTURE OF FAITH. In James 3:6 of the World English Bible it says, *and the tongue is a fire. The world of iniquity among our members is the tongue, which defiles the whole body, and sets on fire the course of nature, and is set on fire by Gehenna and Proverbs 18:21 Death and life are in the power of the tongue; those who love it will eat its fruit.* We must speak life to counteract those dead things spoken over us and by us. God has given us power and authority to speak those things that are not as though they were and we can speak of healing. As a person thinks so are they, think healed. Let this mind be in you which was also in Christ Jesus when He said never-the-less not my will but Your will be done.

He has also given us binding and loosing power here on earth. Amen

CHAPTER 29

IT IS OK

I was one who said yes, I will go and go. Yes, I do it and do it. Yes! This or that. But when it was my turn, it was crickets. At first it hurt, then I got upset. I would still be there anyway and do it anyway. But the past years. I have learned through God not to be bitter but to become better. It is okay to say; "NO." It is okay not to be invited, it is okay not to invite and it is okay if they are a no show. You see it is not about me, you, or them, it is about God getting the glory. Knowing that all things work together for the good of those who love God and who are called according to God's purpose according to Romans 8:28.

Sometimes it may be the same ones who sabotage or hinder you that is why God did not allow them to come.

Matthew 9:18-19 *While he told these things to them, behold, a ruler came and worshiped Him, saying, "My daughter has just died, but come and lay your hand on her, and she will live." Jesus got up and followed him, as did His disciples.*

Mark 5:22-24 *Behold, one of the rulers of the synagogue, Jairus by name, came; and seeing Him, he fell at His feet, and begged Him much, saying, "My little daughter is at the point of death. Please come and lay your hands on her, that she may be made healthy, and live." He went with him, and a great multitude followed Him, and they pressed upon Him on all sides.* Let us get to verse thirty-five to forty-three in the same chapter. *While He was still speaking, people came from the synagogue ruler's house saying, "Your daughter is dead. Why bother the Teacher anymore?" But Jesus, when he heard the message spoken, immediately said to the ruler of the synagogue, "**Don't be afraid, only believe." He allowed no one to follow Him, except Peter, James, and John the brother of James**. He came to the synagogue ruler's house, and He saw an uproar, weeping, and great wailing. **When He had** *entered in, He said to them, "Why do you make an uproar and weep? The child is not dead, but is asleep." They ridiculed Him. But he, having put them all out, took the father of the child, her mother, and those who were with Him, and went in where the child was lying. Taking the child by the hand, He said to her, "Talitha cumi!" which means, being interpreted, "Girl, I tell you, get up!" Immediately the girl rose up and walked, for she was twelve years old. They were amazed with great amazement. He strictly ordered them that no one should know this, and commanded that something should be given to her to eat.* This Scripture is also found in Luke 8:40-56.

We are to love everyone but everyone is not meant to go or be there. Scriptures tell us we must be led by the Spirit. Therefore, if we are following His lead then it is okay not to be everywhere and not to support everyone in everything because the Holy Spirit did not lead us to.

Just like we have the right to ask, leave room for a person to say; Yes or No and be okay with their answer without being upset with them. God gives us a free will but humankind wants to back each other up into a corner to make them say yes. Allow God's Holy Spirit to use you.

We must make sure that we hear God clearly when He says go, stay, or wait. It is His voice we must obey and our obedience to Him is better than making foolish sacrifices.

CHAPTER 30

WHAT SPIRIT

We must pray at all times in the Spirit with the Spirit. There are many kinds of spirits. I will briefly touch on a few. The human spirit notices it is a lower-case (s) and the Holy Spirit is an upper-case (S). There is a way that seems right to humankind but the end leads to a different unexpected turn and that turn is death and destruction according to Proverbs 14:12. The first is spiritual death then eventually natural death.

People will argue their case and what they believe in until the very end. Everyone believes they are right in their own eyes in Proverbs 21:2. And it is not about use and whose right or wrong it is about God and His Word. Paraphrasing Romans 3:4 "Let God's word be true and every man(kind's) word a liar" Not that every person lies but if it does not line up with the word of God it is a lie.

They who win souls are wise in Proverbs 11:30. Winning souls requires us to do it God's way and not our own. We must be wise as a serpent but harmless as a dove according to Matthew 10:16. We are not to use certain tactics like control, manipulation, intimidation, domination, or such like things. We can turn others away from the gospel of Jesus the Christ.

Share the unadulterated Word of God and let the God of the Word perform it. He is faithful over His word and it will not return to Him void it will be carried out wherever He sends it. Many times, people operate on their motives. There are times when others may have wrong feelings of their motives. Trying to get others to see our views the way we see them. We sometimes operate without the Spirit of God. When we do this, we go into operation in and with another spirit.

We can also become puffed up with pride based on our knowledge of a particular sin that we are not in or no longer practice. This can cause us to fall into another area of sin. We should not use manipulation, intimidation, or any of the non-Scripture based things not mentioned in this message to control or dominate a situation or the person to do or not to do whatever it is that you want them to do. We are not to have head knowledge only but have it written in our hearts. If we lack wisdom ask God and we ought to use our spirit of discernment that God gave us as believers. Remembering God gave everyone a free will choice to choose or not to choose. We have been given a great commission to share the Gospel of Jesus the Christ and Him crucified. Do not grieve the Holy Spirit be led by Him to say what the Lord says. If they do not receive the words then shake the dust from your feet and let your peace return to you and move on.

CHAPTER 31

THe SPiRiT Of GOD PRays

Sometimes when we do not know how to pray or do not want to pray all we have to do is open our mouth. Saying something to God just began to give Him thanks and one thank You leads to another and the Spirit of God takes over.

No matter who prays for us or does not pray for us we have a job to pray. Even when we do not know the right words to say the Spirit of God prays. Romans 8:26-27 *In the same way, the Spirit also helps our weaknesses, for we do not know how to pray as we ought. But the Spirit Himself* (INTERCEDES) *makes intercession for us with groanings which cannot be uttered. He who searches the hearts knows what is on the Spirit's mind, because He makes intercession for the saints according to God.* WEB

The Spirit of God intercedes for God's people in accordance to the will of God.

I have been in spiritual warfare many times and the Holy Spirit takes over and you must follow His lead or you will be off. The Holy Spirit does not always tell us to speak. Many times, He will also tell us not to say a word and we must be quiet. Therefore, we must be quick to listen to the Spirit of God and slow to speak whatever the Lord says. Like in James 1:19 to be quick to listen, slow to speak. This is a good principle in our natural and spiritual life.

One problem is when someone says God's word says this or that. But will skip self like God does not speak directly to the speaker first. Many times, we must not be so quick to pick up the phone or run and tell others. Also, leaders must put the microphone down as we all must first look in the mirror. Like a verse in the book of James says when you walk away you forget. James 1:24 *for he sees himself, and goes away, and immediately forgets what kind of man he was.* _{WEB}

So, we must look deep within our soul which is our mind, will and emotions. We must search our mind, will and emotions to see if we are in the flesh or in the spirit. We must allow the Spirit of God to lead us. Otherwise, we will be speaking but not saying anything to glorify our God. Allow the words coming out of our mouths to speak oracles of God. So that it can even speak to our own sinful flesh. The words or prophecy spoken may or may not be for the people but for that person in the mirror. Or it could be for the people or a certain person but we must examine it. 1 John 4:1 *Beloved, do not believe every spirit, but test the spirits, whether they are of God, because many false prophets have gone out into the world.* _{WEB}

CHAPTER 32

CHASE GOD

Jeremiah 14:14 *Then Yahweh said to me, the prophets prophesy lies in my name; I did not send them, neither have I commanded them, neither spoke I to them: they prophesy to you a lying vision, and divination, and a thing of nothing, and the deceit of their own heart.* WEB

Many run here and there chasing prophets for a word. Stop chasing after people and a word. Do not be so quick to send your message to that person who you think it is for. Do not quickly jump on Facebook to write that post or pick up the telephone etc. Let the Word of God find you. The prophecy is already written in the Holy Scriptures. Anything prophecy contrary to what is written is of the person or the devil. Galatians 1:8 *But even though we, or an angel from heaven, should preach to you any "good news" other than that which we preached to you, let him be cursed.* WEB

GOD SAY THEY PROPHECY BUT HE DID NOT SEND THEM. MANY CALL THEMSELVES PROPHETS AND PROPHETESS ARE OPERATING UNDER THE SPIRIT OF DIVINATION. Jeremiah 23:21 *I sent not these prophets, yet they ran: I did not speak to them, yet they prophesied.* WEB

WE MUST NOT TOLERATE THE SPIRIT OF JEZEBEL ANY LONGER OR GOD WILL DEAL WITH US. Revelation 2:20 *But I have this against you, that you tolerate your woman, Jezebel, who calls herself a prophetess. She teaches and seduces my servants to commit sexual immorality, and to eat things sacrificed to idols.* WEB

According to Revelation 2:23 God searches the minds and hearts of everyone and He will give to each one according to our deeds.

Ephesians 5:7 warns us not to BE PARTAKERS IN NO ONE EVIL DEED. It doesn't matter who they are or what title they have. Many who will say Lord, Lord will not enter into His Kingdom. He said: Why call Me Lord and do not do the things I say. He also said; many honor Him with their lips but their heart is far from Him.

According to 2 Timothy 3:16 Every *Scripture is God-breathed and profitable for teaching, for reproof, for correction, and for instruction in righteousness.* WEB

God made sure He left Scripture for us so that we would learn and have hope according to Romans 15:4 *For whatever things were written before were written for our learning, that through perseverance and through encouragement of the Scriptures we might have hope.* WEB

2 Corinthians 11:13-15 *For such men are false apostles, deceitful workers, masquerading as Christ's apostles. And no wonder, for even Satan masquerades as an angel of light. It is no wonderful thing therefore if his servants also masquerade as servants of righteousness, whose end will be according to their works.* WEB

CHAPTER 33

GOING ALONE WITH GOD

Just because you leave a person, place, or thing. DO NOT mean that you do not love them anymore. It just means that you are not on the same assignment or you are going in different directions. Just remember you cannot take everybody with you when God is doing something in your life. Just like you cannot go everywhere with people when God is doing something in the life of others. Especially if God did not authorize you to go with them or them to go with you.

Everyone has their own course to run. We must run our race and stay in our own lane. It is a dangerous place to cross over into someone else's lanes without God's permission and they are willing or not willing to let you in.

In 1 Corinthians 9:24-27 *Don't you know that those who run in a race all run, but one receives the prize? Run like that, that you may win. Every man who strives in the game's exercises self-control in all things. Now they do it to receive a corruptible crown, but we an incorruptible. I therefore run like that, as not uncertainly. I fight like that, as not beating the air, but I beat my body and bring it into submission, lest by any means, after I have preached to others, I myself should be rejected.* WEB

We must step out on faith even if we do not know the next step. We must endure to the end, fight the fight of faith, and finish our own course. 2 Timothy 4:7 *I have fought the good fight. I have finished the course. I have kept the faith.* WEB

CHAPTER 34

CHANGING PARTNERS

I had often heard people say when they got saved "I changed partners." Meaning they were once on the devil's side now they are on the Lord's side. The problem with changing partners is you become a convert but you have not yet been converted. Some have been saying that 5, 10, 15 plus years of being saved but they still have a lot of their old ways. Many of them are in leadership of some kind. The manifestation of their old ways is often seen when certain situations arouse. Acts 6:3 Therefore *select from among you, brothers, seven men of good report, full of the Holy Spirit and of wisdom, whom we may appoint over this business.* We still must keep them in prayer and in the word of God according to Acs 6:4 *But we will continue steadfastly in prayer and in the ministry of the word.* WEB

In part of what the word says if you are to become an overseer this can stand for in any position found in 1 Timothy 3:6 *not a new convert, lest being puffed up he fall into the same condemnation as the devil.* WEB

The mere fact if you only change partners, you are a convert. Just becoming a convert, it takes a while to become converted. If one never gets converted, they will still be bound in addict-like behaviors long after the addiction is over UNLESS IT'S THE LORD WHO DELIVERS, HEALS & MAKE YOU FREE. I thank God for many being made free & keep praying for self and others. Scripture tells us whom the Son makes or sets free is free indeed.

If we do not get our minds fixed, in other words stay on God. Our minds will always be to and from causing us to waiver. In the World English Bible the book of James, in chapter1 verse six through eight says *but let him ask in faith, without any doubting, for he who doubts is like a wave of the sea, driven by the wind and tossed. For let that man not think that he will receive anything from the Lord. He is a double-minded man, unstable in all his ways.* WEB

If we get our minds stayed on Jesus, He will direct our path and keep us in perfect peace. Even when the enemy would rather us be driven to and from, as he tries to shift us as wheat and devour us. We must know that it will not work. "It won't work." NO WEAPONS FORMED AGAINST ME OR YOU SHALL PROSPER. "IT WON'T WORK!" The weapons may form but it will not do us no harm. Scripture tells us all things, not some things but ALL things work together for the good of them who love the Lord and who are called according to His purpose.

People may look at where you have been. They may look at where you are and still not know your current assignment because their assignment is to try to stop it knowingly or unknowingly. Like when Jesus had to rebuke Peter in Mark 8:33 because he was unknowingly speaking from a human mind set and not spiritual. Man looks at the outward appearance but God looks at the heart. Do you desire to follow God's word for your life? Do you have compassion for others? If not, you may experience some things to finally get it? His word cuts to heal you. Hebrew 4:12 *For the word of God is living, and active, and sharper than any two-edged sword, and piercing even to the dividing of soul and spirit, of both joints and marrow, and is able to discern the thoughts and intentions of the heart.* WEB

If the word of God cuts you it only cuts to heal you. Jesus is the Healing Balm we all need. Once we apply the healing Word of God to our lives healing takes place some immediately and some takes time. The word says by His stripes we are healed. Have faith, do not be afraid and just believe.

CHAPTER 35

TO Be MORe Like HiM

Matthew 10:35 *It is enough for the disciple that he be like his teacher, and the servant like his Lord.* WEB

Jesus heals us to be more like Him and not like them. Who is Him? Jesus/ Yeshua! Who are they? These are the people you admire or look up to. These are the ones that have the biggest influence over your life. Those ones whose words you hold dear or their words keep playing over and over in your head.

2 Peter we are to make our calling sure let us look at verses three to eleven: *seeing that His divine power has granted to us all things that pertain to life and godliness, through the knowledge of Him who called us by His own glory and virtue; by which He has granted to us His precious and exceedingly great promises; that through these you may become partakers of the divine nature, having escaped from the corruption that is in the world by lust. Yes, and for this very cause* **adding on your part all diligence, in your faith supply moral excellence; and in moral excellence, knowledge; and in knowledge, self-control; and in self-control patience; and in patience godliness; and in godliness brotherly affection; and in brotherly affection, love.** *For if these things are yours and abound, they make you to be not idle nor unfruitful to the knowledge of our Lord Jesus Christ. For he who lacks these things is blind, seeing only what is near, having forgotten the cleansing from his old sins. Therefore, brothers, be more diligent to make your calling and election sure. For if you do these things, you will never stumble. For thus you will be richly supplied with the entrance into the eternal Kingdom of our Lord and Savior, Jesus Christ.*

These things can be done according to our faith. We can speak to that mountain and it be removed, we can ask the Father in the name of Jesus. We must have faith because without it we cannot even please

God. First faith to believe that He is and second the faith to believe that He is a rewarder to them who diligently seek. Not seeking Him for what He can do but for who He is. Seeking His Kingdom and all His righteousness. Faith speaks to the obstacles in our lives no matter how big or small they are and believe God. Whatever your mountain is, do not let it speak to you. Tell your mountain about your God and watch your God move it right out of your way or give you strength you need to conquer that mountain. We cannot keep repeating what the enemy has said to us or has shown us. We must lift the name of Jesus the Christ. He said if He be lifted, He will draw all unto Him. In Matthew 5:16 *Even so, let your light shine before men; that they may see your good works, and glorify your Father who is in heaven.* WEB

Jesus was always talking about the Father. Jesus said in John 8:38 of the World English Bible ***I say the things which I have seen with My Father; and you also do the things which you have seen with your father.*** He was talking about His Father and their father the devil.

We must seek the will of our Father, hear His voice and obey in John 5:30 *I can of Myself do nothing. As I <u>hear</u>, I judge, and My judgment is righteous; because **I do not seek my own will, but the <u>will </u>of my Father who sent Me**.* WEB

Brothers and sisters, we inherit things from our natural families. But we have been adopted into God's Royal family and we have a new inheritance. Therefore, we do not have to accept the old inheritance. Behold all things are new because we are a new creation. So that thing that runs in the old-line u do not have to name it or claim it.

Jesus' blood NEVER LOSES ITS POWER.

CHAPTER 36

WHOSE ORDER?

Many people talk about order but most of the time it is just talk. We must be the order that we tell everyone else to be about even when no one else is with you. When you are about the order of God. It makes it possible to then change the atmosphere to be conducive to the Spirit of God. We are called to order by His Spirit and through our obedience to His Spirit. Our words and actions will line up with the will and the word of God.

We follow man-made rules that have nothing to do with the order of God most of our lives. When there is order then ciaos must flee. We will learn and know our own lane and help others and there will be no desire to take anyone's place or there will be no desire to feel like someone is. We will recognize the gifts in operation.

We have enough trouble just being ourselves, the only true person we can be. God is not looking for a copycat, a mini you or another me. Unless we are copying Him, we are not being true to Him or self. When we look for a child of God their life should be hidden in Christ Jesus. That we do not know them after the flesh but after the Spirit. We must do it the way He says to do it and no other way, not even our own. We all must answer to Him now and in the next life for these deeds done in this body. When He looks for me, I do not want Him to find me trying to be someone else, being what you want me to be or doing my own thing.

The devil is an imitator. God is the creator. Just like in Genesis 9:17 *God said to Noah, "This is the token of the covenant which I have established between me and all flesh that is on the earth.* WEB.

God created the rainbow sign as a covenant reminder between earth and Him that He will never destroy the whole earth by flood. What the devil meant for evil God will turn it around for the good of them that love Him and are called according to His purpose. The rainbow signs will remind God of His covenant promise. One day the earth will be destroyed again. But not by a lake of water but by a lake of fire. Revelation 20:14 *Death and Hades were thrown into the lake of fire. This is the second death, the lake of fire.* WEB

God has an order and it is not like mankind's order. Therefore, our will must line up with God's will and not the other way around or no other way.

CHAPTER 37

WHAT DO YOU STAND FOR?

If you do not stand for something you will fall for anything? A kingdom divided by itself cannot stand. There has been a division across the board of events. Now they who caused the division sit back and watch whose side we are on. While we bicker about the smallest trivial matters that we were foretold about throughout the Bible.

While the kingdoms watch and set up the bigger events that you have been ignoring. It is and has been leading to the Antichrist all along. Satan's synagogues. As the world began to wax cold. Matthew 24:9-14 *Then they will deliver you up to oppression, and will kill you. You will be hated by all the nations for my name's sake. Then many will stumble, and will deliver up one another, and will hate one another. Many false prophets will arise, and will lead many astray. Because iniquity will be multiplied, the love of many will grow cold.* **But he or she who endures to the end, the same will be saved.** *This Good News of the Kingdom will be preached in the entire world for a testimony to all the nations, and then the end will come.* WEB

We are to love everyone and if we hate anything that means we are to love it less. We are to hate what God hates, WE ARE NOT TO LOVE ANYONE OR ANYTHING MORE THAN WE LOVE JESUS.

Matthew 10:37-39 *He who loves father or mother more than Me is not worthy of Me; and he who loves son or daughter more than Me is not worthy of Me. He who does not take his cross and follow Me, is not worthy of Me. He who seeks his life will lose it; and he who loses his life for My sake will find it.* WEB

He said bear the cross. He did not say where or what your cross or cost was or will be.

Luke 14:26-33 *If anyone comes to me, and does not disregard his own father, mother, wife, children, brothers, and sisters, yes, and his own life also, he cannot be My disciple. Whoever does not bear his own cross, and come after Me, cannot be My disciple. For which of you, desiring to build a tower, doesn't first sit down and count the cost, to see if he has enough to complete it? Or perhaps, when he has laid a foundation, and is not able to finish, everyone who sees begins to mock him, saying, 'This man began to build, and wasn't able to finish.' Or what king, as he goes to encounter another king in war, will not sit down first and consider whether he is able with ten thousand to meet him who comes against him with twenty thousand? Or else, while the other is yet a great way off, he sends an envoy, and asks for conditions of peace. So therefore, whoever of you who does not renounce all that he has, he cannot be \My disciple.* _{WEB}

I wrote this is a poem:

STAND

United we stand not divided by man

That was not part of our God's plan

One will stand together with the world and its systems like a friend

Instead of seeking the Lord whose government has no end

We must be solid as a rock because it can not bend

His Kingdom is where we will receive our eternal reward

Because He is King of kings and Lord of lords

Here on earth, we must be on one accord

Unified we must stand and separated we will fall

When our time comes we must all answers our call

This world's religion has told it all

We all need Jesus the Christ and nothing more

It is time to stand together like never before

While Christ is still knocking at your door

Either we stand for God because He said what He mean Either we are cold or hot there is no in-between

CHAPTER 38

LETTING GO

There is a difference between letting go and giving up. In Luke 14:33 who does not renounce all that he or she has, they cannot be Jesus' disciples. Did you count the cost in what you have built on? Referring to Luke 14:28 in the earlier chapter. A person building a house, who dug and went deep, and laid a foundation on the rock. When a flood arose, the stream broke against that house, and could not shake it, because it was found on the rock. According to the grace of God which was given to us, as builders on the foundation which was already laid by the will of God and Jesus, others build on it. Therefore, let each one be careful how they build on it.

Many times, we get tired and want to give up. Sometimes it is not always that easy because we have invested so much time and energy and we want to go the last mile. Other times we want to let go but we keep holding on to the what ifs. We often hear the praise "let go and let God." Many may say what does that really mean or how can you know the difference?

As I scrolled looking through my pictures today the smiles and laughs of family together is greater than when the family is apart. Sometimes when we get together the aftermath makes you wish you had not. This does not mean you do not love your family and friends, it just means that you value your peace. So, you let go of the gatherings and not the family. Although many have given up and do not want to be bothered at all. Some may not have any ill feelings towards one another while others are still holding on to the way they feel.

When our children are small and we want them to grow up and once they are grown, we do not want to let them go. Therefore, we let them go but we do not give up. Scripture tells us to train them up in the way they should go. We must let them grow and learn from their own mistakes. We must trust them and God that what you have taught them, they will turn to it when they need to.

All too often we are in a hurry to push each other out of our lives or away from us. Sometimes we miss the blessings because we do not know what is right there in our face until it is grown or gone.

There is a learning lesson for all parties involved.

Therefore, we cannot be so quick to let go or give up. Remember one water and one plant but it is God who gives the increase.

We also must know when to shake the dust off our feet and let our peace return to us. We must also know when we are casting our pearls upon a non-receptive person.

There are times we just must know when to let go. Letting go is not giving up, it is just putting it in God's hands. You may get tired of carrying people who should be standing up and walking on their own two feet. So, you just let go and let God, it does not mean that you do not love them. You just must stop handicapping them, being their crutch and enabler. We must be willing to give them tough love so they can grow and go.

The foundation is in Jesus Christ and allows His Spirit to lead you into when to let go and keep on serving Him.

CHAPTER 39

WHY SETTLE

God has His perfect will for our lives. Just because we want what we want we will settle for His permissive will. Why? Because we do not want to wait on the Lord.

A man will settle with the one he gets, until he works to get the one he wants. Why because a man is visual and he goes by what he sees. And he is intellectual and he will use his head to plan to achieve his goal. Let us see how Jacob wanted the youngest daughter and the dad planned to marry the oldest daughter first to their custom. We will see how both men achieved their goal and got what they wanted. Let us read Genesis 29:15-30 *Laban said to Jacob, "Because you are my brother, should you therefore serve me for nothing?* **Tell me, what will your wages be?"** *Laban had two daughters. The name of the elder was Leah, and the name of the younger was Rachel. Leah's eyes were weak, but Rachel was beautiful in form and attractive. Jacob loved Rachel. He said, "***I will serve you seven years for Rachel,*** your younger daughter." Laban said, "It is better that I give her to you, than that I should give her to another man. Stay with me."* **Jacob served seven years for Rachel.** *They seemed to him but a few days, for the love he had for her. Jacob said to Laban, "Give me my wife, for my days are fulfilled, that I may go in to her." Laban gathered together all the men of the place, and* **made a feast.** *It happened in the evening, that he took* **Leah** *his daughter, and brought her to him. He went in to her. Laban gave Zilpah his handmaid to his daughter Leah for a handmaid. It happened in the morning that, behold, it was Leah. He said to Laban, "***What is this you have done to me? Didn't I serve with you for Rachel? Why then have you deceived me?"*** *Laban said, "It is not done so in our place, to give the younger before the firstborn. Fulfill the week of this one, and we will give you the other also for the service which you will* **serve with me yet seven other years."** *Jacob did so, and fulfilled her week.* **He gave him Rachel his daughter as wife.** *Laban gave to Rachel his daughter Bilhah, his handmaid, to be her handmaid.* **He** *went in also to Rachel, and he also loved Rachel more than Leah, and served with him yet seven other years.*

A man can have many children with you & never love you. Learn to Love God more and dedicate your children to Him lets continue and read Genesis 29:31-35 **Yahweh saw that Leah was hated, and he opened her womb, but Rachel was barren.** Leah conceived, and bore a son, and she named him Reuben. For she said, "Because Yahweh has looked at my affliction. For now, my husband will love me." She conceived again, and bore a son, and said, "Because Yahweh has heard that I am hated, he has therefore given me this son also." She named him Simeon. She conceived again, and bore a son. Said, "Now this time will my husband be joined to me, because I have borne him three sons." Therefore, was his name called Levi. She conceived again, and bore a son. She said, "This time will I praise Yahweh." Therefore, she named him Judah. Then she stopped bearing.

The woman can love a man so much until she loose herself and her relationship with God. You see in Scripture God did not have to tell the woman to love her husband but He told the man to love His wife. 1 Peter 3:7 *You husbands, in the same way, live with your wives according to knowledge, giving honor to the woman, as to the weaker vessel, as being also joint heirs of the grace of life; **that your prayers may not be hindered**.* WEB

A woman is emotional and she thinks with her heart. She does not always go by what she sees but she will go by what she feels and what a man says to her. She will love her children and her husband. Sometimes so much they forget about God and you see here in the Scripture above how she praised God each time she had a son not for God being God but her affections and focus was on her and her husband. When she had the fourth son, she praised God and her son's name means praise and she stopped conceiving.

Single women and married women's interests are different. Single women, keep yourselves for the Lord's use.

1 Corinthians 7:34 *There is also a difference between a wife and a virgin. The unmarried woman cares about the things of the Lord, that she may be holy both in body and in spirit. But she who is married cares about the things of the world--how she may please her husband.* WEB

1 Peter 3:1 *In the same way, wives, be in subjection to your own husbands; so that, even if any do not obey the Word, they may be won by the behavior of their wives without a word; seeing your pure behavior in fear. Let your beauty be not just the outward adorning of braiding the hair, and of wearing jewels of gold, or of putting on fine clothing; but in the hidden person of the heart, in the incorruptible adornment of a gentle and quiet spirit, which is in the sight of God very precious. For this is how the holy women before, who hoped in God also adorned themselves, being in subjection to their own husbands: 6as Sarah obeyed Abraham, calling him lord, whose children you now are, if you do well, and are not put in fear by any terror.* WEB

CHAPTER 40

WHERE THERE IS NO REBUKE

Many times we need to be rebuked or we may need to rebuke others. A rebuke does not always feel good but it is necessary. A rebuke is a strong disagreement.

When dealing with false teachers Titus 1:13-16 *This testimony is true. For this cause, **reprove them sharply**, that they may be sound in the faith, not paying attention to Jewish fables and commandments of men who turn away from the truth. To the pure, all things are pure; but to those who are defiled and unbelieving, nothing is pure; but both their mind and their conscience are defiled. They profess that they know God, but by their works they deny Him, being abominable, disobedient, and unfit for any excellent work.* WEB

My problem is not the rebuke, it is where there is no reprove. where there is no rebuke. Jesus rebuked Peter in Mark 8:33 There is a problem when everyone is allowed to do any and everything especially the ones in leadership or in the body are manifest, these adultery, fornication, strange flesh, lasciviousness, idolatry, witchcraft, hatred, wrath, strife, envying, murders, drunkenness, and such like.

When someone sins it is better to rebuke them without delay according to 1 Timothy 5:20 *Those who sin, **reprove in the sight of all, that the rest also may be in fear.*** WEB

We cannot refuse to rebuke someone because we love them. According to Proverb 27:5 *Better is open rebuke than hidden love.* WEB

God does not show partiality and neither should we.
Romans 2:11 *For there is no partiality with God* and
James 2:1 *My brothers* (sister), *do not hold the faith of our Lord Jesus Christ of glory with.* WEB

In Luke 17:3-4 *Be careful if your brother* or sister *sins against you,* **rebuke him. If he repents, forgive him.** *If he sins against you seven times in the day, and seven times returns, saying, 'I repent,' you shall forgive him.* _{WEB}

There is a cost of following Jesus found in Scripture. Let us see in Luke 9:57 *As they went on the way, a certain man said to Him, "I want to follow you wherever you go, Lord." Jesus said to him, "The foxes have holes, and the birds of the sky have nests, but **the Son of Man has no place to lay His head." He said** to another, "Follow me!" But he said, "Lord, allow me first to go and bury my father." But Jesus said to him, "**Leave the dead to bury their own dead, but you go and announce the Kingdom of God."** Another also said, "I want to follow you, Lord, **but first allow me to say good-bye to those who are at my house."** But Jesus said to him, "**No one, having put his hand to the plow, and looking back, is fit for the Kingdom of God."***

Do not be deceived, we have to take up our cross and deny ourselves to follow Christ found in *Matthew 16:24-27 Then Jesus said to His disciples, "If anyone desires to come after Me, let him deny himself, and take up his cross, and follow Me. For whoever desires to save his life will lose it, and whoever will lose his life for My sake will find it. For what will it profit a man, if he gains the entire world, and forfeits his life? Or what will a man give in exchange for his life? For the Son of Man will come in the glory of his Father with his angels, and then he will render to everyone according to his deeds* When Jesus predicted His death and resurrection, Peter tried to rebuke Jesus. Jesus had to rebuke His own disciple, Peter in Mark 8:31-33 *He began to teach them that the Son of Man must suffer many things, and be rejected by the elders, the chief priests, and the scribes, and be killed, and after three days rise again. He spoke to them openly. **Peter took Him, and began to rebuke Him.***

But he, turning around, and seeing His disciples, rebuked Peter, *and said, "Get behind me, Satan! For you have in mind not the things of God, but the things of men."* _{WEB}

2 Timothy 3:16 *Every Scripture is God-breathed and profitable for teaching, for reproof, for correction, and for instruction in righteousness, that the man of God may be complete, thoroughly equipped for every excellent work.* _{WEB}

Some of the obstacles can get in the way of us doing the will of God. And we may need to rebuke or correct one another in the Word of God.

In Job 32 of the World English Bible, Elihu Rebukes Job's Three Friends here in verses one to five: **So, these three men ceased to answer Job, because he was righteous in his own eyes.** *Then the wrath of Elihu the son of Barachel, the Buzite, of the family of Ram, was kindled against Job. His wrath was kindled because he justified himself rather than God. Also, his wrath was kindled against his three friends, because they had found no answer, and yet had condemned Job. Now Elihu had waited to speak to Job because they were elder than he. When Elihu saw that there was no answer in the mouth of these three men, his wrath was kindled. In the next chapter he rebukes Job according to Scripture.*

When God tells us to do or say something. We are to do it age do not matter just do it in respect in the way you are told to do it.

We are not to be afraid to be a witness for the Lord. We must not deny Jesus according to Matthew 10:32-33 *Everyone therefore who confesses Me before men, him I will also confess before My Father who is in heaven. But whoever denies Me before men, him I will also deny before My Father who is in heaven.* _{WEB}

We will have troubles in our own household but we must still love God more to do His will. He divided the love that we have for one another that we love Him more than anyone. Matthew 10:34-38 Don't *think that I came to send peace on the earth. I did not come to send peace, but a sword. For I came to set people at odds against his father, and a daughter against her mother, and a daughter-in-law against her mother-in-law. A man's and woman's foes will be those of his and her own household.* **He or she who loves father or mother more than me is not worthy of Me; and he who loves son or daughter more than Me is not worthy of Me. He who does not take his cross and follow after Me, is not worthy of Me.**

We must not be hard headed and are constantly being rebuked. Proverbs 29:1 *He who is often rebuked and stiffens his neck will be destroyed suddenly, with no remedy.* _{WEB}.

None of us is above rebuke NATHAN REBUKED DAVID. We ought not be asking others if this or that is okay to do. Especially when you know what the Word of God says concerning that which you ask. If you do or do not know, just go to the Word of God, and ask the God of the Word. Pray to God and ask him, His will concerning those matters.

Just because everyone else is doing it DO NOT MEAN IT'S OKAY TO DO ESPECIALLY IF YOU WANT GOD TO REALLY USE YOU.

if YOU aRe HURTiNG

Psalm 51:17 *The sacrifices of God are a broken spirit. A broken and contrite heart, O God, you will not despise.* _{WEB}

If you are hurting, it is time to get healed because hurt people really do hurt people. It is time to get better and not bitter. We can be healed through the love and power of Jesus the Christ.

We must be freed in every area of our lives. Some have been hurting so long to pain, it feels like a normal part of their lives. Some keep wondering when this cycle will end. Others do not even know they are in a vicious cycle.

Letting someone go does not mean replacing them with someone else. In doing that you will find that it is just a different face but same or similar spirit. To truly be free we must seek God for your freedom with Jesus. John 8:36 *If therefore the Son makes you free, you will be free indeed.* _{WEB}

If one does not get healed, one will be the victim for way too long. They will also hurt people in one way or another and not realize that they too are part of the problem and solution. With Christ we can go from victim to victor, we are victorious in Him.

The act of the hurts we play repeatedly in our mind. Then we use blockers to try to stop these events from attacking us mentally. Sometimes we can push them so far back in our subconscious mind. When we do that, it is like it never happened. Many times we cover our pain up with substance abuse. The problem when we do this is we never get a chance to face it head on before we become addicted. Each time that pain reappears we run to the blockers. The blockers will relieve the thoughts of it or relieve the pain of the thoughts of it. When it only relieves some of the pain and not the thought, we begin to talk about what has occurred. It is not until we get healed, delivered, and set free by the love and power of the Lord we will be healed. In Jeremiah of the World English Bible chapter seventeen verse fourteen says *Heal me, O Yahweh, and I will be healed. Save me, and I will be saved; for you are my praise and Exodus 15:26 for I am Yahweh who heals you. Isaiah 53:5 says by His stripes we are healed and 1 Peter 2:24 tells us we were healed by His wounds.* It is by Jesus stripes and His wounds He endured for us on the cross. He is our healing Balm; we must apply Him to our wounds and hurts.

What is the nature of your wound? Many times, we must identify when or where the hurt is in our lives. For us to do this we have to face it with a clear mind. If there is substance abuse involved. When one is using some sort of substance and when they try to stop, for many reasons everything gets worse before it gets better. We will deal with one reason. We are standing face to face with what caused us to hurt in our lives and we must now deal with it. We are no longer hiding behind or in the substance to escape.

When we are no longer using the escape. We return to the age when we start using. No not physically but in the other areas such as mentally, emotionally, spiritually. Now we must grow into maturity without the substance. For example, if you started numbing the pain at the age of 15 and you are now 30. Now you are acting like a 15-year-old in a 30-year-old body. Sometimes it takes the same amount of time to heal as it took to suppress it. It is important to tell the people in your household and around you because this will take love and support. Most of all you are doing this for you even if you do not have it.

A big step in this is to forgive who hurt you and forgive yourself if that is necessary. Forgiving others does not excuse what they did to you. Forgiving them is for you; it keeps you from holding what they did hostage in your mind and heart. That is a place that is reserved for God not them. Once you release them you can let God in to fill that space. If they want forgiveness, they must seek it for themselves. God has no respect for people. In Luke 23:34 Jesus said, "Father, forgive them."

Afterward you can get to a place where you too can say those words. I have now gotten to that place and believe me it takes His Spirit in me every single time.

There are many sicknesses and spiritually rooted diseases tied up to our emotions and we must let them go. Letting them go is beneficial to our natural health. Do you see that our emotions agree with the lies of the enemy and it keeps us from forgiving? The enemy operates using our mind, will and emotions. However, when our mind, will and emotions line up with the Word of God we will have faith, trust, and believe Him in Spirit and in Truth.

One of my firsthand experiences when the Lord Himself delivered me. I had started going to a professional counselor. After several weeks she said to me "I know we are not supposed to talk about God but since you talk about Him so much, I am just going to say this I can't help you." I asked, why? She replied "What I was supposed to do, your God has already done." She also said "I will no longer be working here and if you feel like you still need counseling there will be a counselor for you." I never went back.

I am not giving medical advice in any part of this book. If you require medical advice, please see your doctors. In some cases, a person may need additional medical help, some type counseling or therapy. If so, there is nothing wrong with getting whatever help is needed.

In other matters it could be a case of demon possession and demons are real. This happens when we leave our wounds open, this is an open door for the enemy. Self-medicating also gives the enemy access. A lot of times people want to beat it out especially in children and this does not work. We cannot medicate a demon out nor can we beat one out. Demons must be expelled out.

Ephesians 6:12 *For our wrestling is not against flesh and blood*, *but against the principalities, against the powers, against the world's rulers of the darkness of this age, and against the spiritual forces of wickedness in the heavenly places.* WEB

We do not have time to argue, fight and play with the enemy. Many times we are sleeping with the same enemy we are at war with. Other times the enemy is the "inner me". We spend so much time fighting for our lives and others.

Ephesians 6:10-11 Finally, **be strong in the Lord and in the strength of his might**. Put on the whole armor of God, **that you may be able to stand against the schemes of the devil.** WEB

If you do not know His voice one must pray and get in a relationship with God. You must study the Word of God for yourself and learn directly from Him. Once you receive Him, invite His Spirit in and He will help you. If you do not know or go to the word of God for yourself you will always follow the enemy and the "inner me" or them and NOT HIM. John 10:27 *My sheep hear My voice, and I know them, and they follow Me* WEB.

The moment we start putting confidence in our own flesh we have lost the spiritual battle from a place of victory. The moment we start looking at the person instead of the spirit behind the person we have lost the spiritual battle. Our battles are fought through God. We must get rid of those things in our minds that go against Him. In 2 Corinthians 10:3-6 *for though we walk in the flesh, we do not wage war according to the flesh; for the weapons of our warfare are not of the flesh, but mighty before God to the throwing down of strongholds, throwing down imaginations and every high thing that is exalted against the knowledge of God, and bringing every thought into captivity to the obedience of Christ; and being in readiness to avenge all disobedience, when your obedience will be made full.* WEB

This is a Poem I wrote:

GOD

When you are on assignment from God you cannot worry about things going on around you,

It is time to do what you were assigned to do. This is the time to stay focused on the task at hand, There is much work to do in this land.

We are to watch as well as pray,

We are to walk by faith and not by sight every day.

There are people stuck in bondage seeking to be free. Jesus says I am standing with open arms but they never seek Me.

I am the same God yesterday, today & forever more, I will do it again & again like I did it before.

Yet! You put other gods before Me and call it love, And refer to Me as "the man above".

Have not I proven Myself to you time after time?

I am sublime.

There are no other gods before or after Me.

It is not my hand you should seek when it is My face you will see.

You come to Me more than you give.

Through My grace and mercy, I let you live.

Some make excuses for being in bondage while others blame Me.

I sent My Son that you may have life and not only life but it more abundantly.

I chose you and you did not choose Me,

There are some who received Me and I healed, delivered, and set them free.

Live to live again.

I am sending My Son soon My friend.

CHAPTER 42

TRAiN UP

Proverb 22:6 *Train up a child in the way he* or she *should go, and when he* or she *is old, he will not depart from it.* _{WEB}

Jesus said in Mark 10:15 *Most certainly I tell you, whoever will not receive the Kingdom of God* **like a little child,** *he* or she *will in no way enter into it.* _{WEB}

This is how we are to obey God, like a child is supposed to obey their parents.

Train up your child in the way they should go. They may go astray but they will return to what they were taught early in life. Even as adult children we fall short of our heavenly Fathers glory.

There will be a new worldly system coming that the children of God will not fit in or join. Nevertheless, some children will fall into it. They are falling into the hands of worldly leadership instead of spiritual ones. There is a way that seems right unto humankind but leads up to destruction.

When we are tempted to go astray our God makes a way to escape out of every temptation. Our god will never tempt us with evil although we are tested by God. When that time comes, we will not depart from the training.

Amen

Let us take a glance at The Parable of the Prodigal Son found in Luke 15:11-32 *He said, A certain man had two sons. The younger of them said to his father, 'Father, give me my share of your property. He divided his* *livelihood between them. Few days later, the younger son gathered all of this together and traveled into a far country.* His son departed with ALL his possessions. *There he wasted his property with riotous living.* He spent his money on the things he wanted to spend it on. *When he had spent all of it, there arose a severe famine in that country, and he began to be in need.* After he had spent all that he had, now he does not have money. There became a shortage in the land and he really needed that which he had so carelessly blew. *He went and joined himself to one of the citizens of that country, and he sent him into his fields to feed pigs. He wanted to fill his belly with the husks that the pigs ate, but no one gave him any. But when he came to himself, he said, 'How many hired servants of my fathers have bread enough to spare, and I'm dying with hunger! I will get up and go to my father, and will tell him, "Father, I have sinned against heaven, and in your sight. I am no more worthy to be called your son. Make me as one of your hired servants. He arose, and came to his father. But while he was still far off, his father saw him, and was moved with compassion, and ran, and fell on his neck, and kissed him.* The son said to him, Father, I have sinned against heaven, and in your sight. I am no longer worthy to be called your son. But the father said to his servants, **bring out the best robe, and put it on him. Put a ring on his hand, and shoes on his feet. Bring the fattened calf, kill it, and let us eat, and celebrate; for this, my son, was dead, and is alive again. He was lost, and is found. They began to celebrate.** Now his elder son was in the field. As he came near to the house, he heard music and dancing. He called one of the servants to him, and asked what was going on. He said to him, your brother has come, and your father has killed the fattened calf, because he has received him back safe and healthy. But he was angry, and would not go in. Therefore, his father came out, and begged him. But he answered his father, Behold, these many years I have served you, and I never disobeyed a commandment of yours, but you never gave me a goat, that I might celebrate with my friends. But when this, your son, came, who has devoured your living with prostitutes, you killed the fattened calf for him. He said to him, Son, you are always with me, and all that is mine is yours. **But it was appropriate to celebrate and be glad, for this, your brother, was dead, and is alive again. He was lost, and was found.*** WEB

Our Father in Heaven loves us much more than we will ever know. He is waiting to receive us with open arms.

When His backsliding children return to Him all of heaven angels rejoice over one sinner who repents.

The parable we just read is a wonderful example of the Fathers Love for His children. When we as adults are trained as a child of God because we are babies in Him. Is the same way we are to instruct our children when they are young. they may remain in God, go astray, and may even mess up. No matter how far off they stray away they will always remember the way they were taught. When they remember, they will return to the Lord when all else fails.

When they are babes we must be mindful of what we are sharing, whether in the natural or in the spirit in1 Peter 2:1-3 of the World English Bible *Putting away therefore all wickedness, all deceit, hypocrisies, envies, and all evil speaking, **as newborn babies, long for the pure milk of the Word, that you may grow thereby, if indeed you have tasted that the Lord is gracious.***

When we are mature or full-grown adults, it is time for the meat of the Word of God, if we continue in the milk of the Word, it stunts our growth. Hebrews 5:11-13 is a warning against drifting away: *About him we have many words to say, and hard to interpret, **seeing you have become dull of hearing. For although by this time you should be teachers, you again need to have someone teach you the rudiments of the first principles of the oracles of God. You have come to need milk, and not solid food. For everyone who lives on milk is not experienced in the word of righteousness, for he is a baby. But solid food is for those who are full grown, who by reason of use have their senses exercised to discern good and evil.*** WEB

What are we sharing with others?

What are we sharing with our children and grandchildren?

Are we sharing the unadulterated gospel of Jesus Christ?

Are we instructing our children or sitting them in front of the television, allowing them to play video games all day or giving them some form of electronics?

Are you passing down the me, myself, and I version of what you want to teach them or generational traditions?

Are you sharing something you heard someone else say and their version of the truth?

Do we have time for them or are we always sending them away?

Are we telling them to go play or go sit down?

We may even say to them not now or later and later never comes.

It is one thing to be taught something all your life. Then to finally grow up & learn the truth. But once you learn the truth.

Will you embrace the truth?

Will you still believe the lie?

Will you do your own research and decide for yourself?

We must know that a half-truth is a whole lie. Remember Satan came as an angel of light to Eve in the Garden of Eden, and to Jesus on a mountain presenting a half-truth and a half lie. Therefore, Satan knows the word of God and he will also come to us as an angle of light. There are many wolves in sheep's clothing masquerading to be something that they are not. So, we must be prayerful and careful who we allow to train up our children. Likewise, we also must be watchful on who is leading us. We must become spiritually mature enough to get ourselves out of the way. We must be humble enough to remain teachable. We must know that we can do nothing without God and we need Him. We need His Spirit to help us in our weaknesses.

He has also given us spiritual gifts to help us as well as others in particular areas. Most important He has given every born-again believer His Holy Spirit. We are obligated to study to show ourselves approved unto God. The only one who will be able to give an account for us is ourselves. We must become trained like a child and learn from God. As we learn from Him, we must instruct our children as well as others.

Just as our natural father disciplines his children so does our Heavenly Father. Hebrews 12:4-12 *You have not yet resisted to blood, striving against sin; and you have forgotten the exhortation which reasons with you as with children,* **"My son, don't take lightly the chastening of the Lord, nor faint when you are reproved by Him; For whom the Lord loves, he chastens, and scourges every son whom He receives."** *It is for discipline that you endure. God deals with you as with children, for what son is there whom his father does not discipline? But if you are without discipline, of which all have been made partakers, then are you illegitimate, and not children. Furthermore, we had the fathers of our flesh to chasten us, and we paid them respect. Shall we not much be in subjection to the Father of spirits, and live? For they indeed, for a few days, punished us as seemed good to them; but He for our profit, that we may be partakers of His holiness. All chastening seems for the present to be not joyous but grievous; yet afterward it yields the peaceful fruit of righteousness to those who have been exercised thereby.* Therefore, lift the hands that hang down and the feeble knees, and make straight paths for your feet, so that which is lame may not be dislocated, **but be healed.** _{WEB}

CHAPTER 43

SOWING AND GIVING

Sowing is a spiritual principle and is not consistent with money, it is pertaining to the Word of God. Look at this parable of the sower found in Luke 8:5-15 *The farmer went out to sow his seed. As he sowed, some fell along the road, and it was trampled underfoot, and the birds of the sky devoured it. Other seed fell on the rock, and as soon as it grew, it withered away, because it had no moisture Other fell amid the thorns, and the thorns grew with it, and choked it. Other fell into the good ground, and grew, and brought forth fruit one hundred times. As He said these things, He called out, "He who has ears to hear, let him hear!" Then His disciples asked Him, what does this parable mean? He said, to you it is given to know the mysteries of the Kingdom of God, but to the rest in parables; that seeing they may not see, and hearing they may not understand. Now the parable is this: **The seed is the word of God. Those along the road are those who hear, then the devil comes, and takes away the word from their heart, that they may not believe and be saved. Those on the rock are they who, when they hear, receive the word with joy; but these have no root, who believe for a while, then fall away in time of temptation. That which fell among the thorns, these are those who have heard, and as they go on their way they are choked with cares, riches, and pleasures of life, and bring no fruit to maturity. That in the good ground, these are such as in an honest and good heart, having heard the word, hold it tightly, and bring forth fruit with patience.* _{WEB}

Another account of Jesus explains the parable of the sower is found in Matthew 13:18-23 *Hear, then, the parable of the farmer. When anyone hears **the word of the Kingdom**, and does not understand it, the evil one comes, and snatches away that which has been sown in his heart. This is what was sown by the roadside. What was sown on the rocky places, this is he who hears the word, and immediately with joy receives it; yet he has no root in himself, but endures for a while. When oppression or persecution arises because of the word, immediately he stumbles. What was sown among the thorns, this is he who* *hears the word, but the cares of this age and the deceitfulness of riches choke the word, and he becomes unfruitful. What was sown on the good ground, this is he who hears the word, and understands it, who most certainly bears fruit, and brings forth, some one hundred times as much, some sixty, and some thirty.* _{WEB}

Another account of Jesus explaining the seed and sower found in Mark 4:13-20 *He said to them, "Don't you understand this parable? How will you understand all the parables? **The farmer sows the word**. The ones by the road are the ones **where the word is sown**; and when they have heard, **immediately Satan comes, and takes away the word which has been sown in them**. These in the same way are those who are sown on the rocky places, who, when they have heard the word, immediately receive it with joy. They have **no root** in themselves, but are short-lived. When oppression or persecution arises **because of the word**, immediately they **stumble**. Others are those who are sown among the thorns. These are those who have heard the word, and **the cares of** this age, and the deceitfulness of riches, and the lusts of other things entering in **choke the word**, and it becomes unfruitful. Those which were **sown on the good ground** are those who hear the word, and accept it, and bear fruit, some thirty times, some sixty times, and some one hundred times.* _{WEB}

Sowing is not monetary gifts as many believe in fact the best seed we can sow is the Word of God. Now in reference to giving on the other hand is related to money as well as other things. Just because you have the monetary resources does not mean you have to give it right there. Seek God on how and where He wants you to give financially. We will reap what we sow but not necessarily where we sow it. The same principle is in our giving. Luke 6:38 *Give, and it will be given to you: good measure, pressed down, shaken together, and running over, will be given to you. For with the same measure, you measure it will be measured back to you.* _{WEB}

*Now we may sow spiritually but reap naturally Paul the Apostle wrote in 1 Corinthians 9:11-14 If we **sowed to you spiritual things, is it a wonderful thing if we reap your fleshly things?** If others partake of this right over you, don't we yet more? Nevertheless, we did not use this right, but we bear all things, that we may cause no hindrance to the Good News of Christ. Don't* *you know that those who serve around sacred things eat from the things of the temple, and those who wait on the altar have their portion with the altar?* **Even so the Lord ordained that those who proclaim the Good News should live from the Good News.** _{WEB}

Galatians 6:6 **But let him who is taught in the word share all good things with him who teaches.** *Do not be deceived. God is not mocked, for whatever a man sows, that he will also reap. For he who sows to his own flesh will from the flesh reap corruption.* **But he who sows to the Spirit will from the Spirit reap eternal life. Let us not be weary in doing good, for we will reap in due season, if we do not give up. So then, as we have opportunity, let us do what is good toward all men, and especially toward those who are of the household of the faith.** _{WEB}

Here in this Scripture is the spiritual principle of sowing, reaping, and giving as mentioned in 2 Corinthians 9:6 *Remember this: he who sows sparingly will also reap sparingly. He who sows bountifully will also reap bountifully.* **Let each person give according as he or she has determined in his or her heart**; *not grudgingly, or under compulsion; for God loves a cheerful giver. And God is able to make all grace abound to you, that you, always having all sufficiency in everything, may abound to every excellent work.* _{WEB}

According to Scripture giving and sowing is a hearts condition on how we reap. We must not give grudgingly, resentful or in a reluctant way. We are not to give under compulsion, out of obligation, pressure, intimidation, or force of any kind.

What seems good to us may not be good to God. It is said every good thing is not a God thing but every God thing is a good thing not just concerning giving but in everything we do. When the poor woman gave the two small brass coins which was all she had and the others gave much, out of their abundance found in Mark 12:41-44 and Luke 21:1-4.

We must sow on good ground to reap a harvest from God. We will reap a harvest in due season if we do not faint in our sowing season. If we sow sparingly, we will reap sparingly; if we sow bountifully, we will reap bountifully in a due season. Give and it shall be given unto us a good measure pressed down shaken together and running over will He (God) cause humankind to give to us. The Most High does use human participants here on this earth in His miracles.

Just because we know how to sow and give does not mean it from God. Wisdom tells us much more about our sowing and giving. All we must do is ask God for wisdom according to Scripture in the book of James. We all need to pray and ask God for wisdom on who, what, when, where and how to give and sow. Give and sow not just in our own house, friends and family but give and so that others may be blessed too.

Let us look at the parable of the rich fool in Luke 12:13-21 *One of the multitudes said to Him, "Teacher, tell my brother to divide the inheritance with me." But He said to him, "Man, who made me a judge or an arbitrator over you?" He said to them, "Beware!* **Keep yourselves from covetousness**, *for a man's life doesn't consist of the abundance of the things which he possesses." He spoke a parable to them, saying, "The ground of a certain rich man brought forth abundantly. He reasoned within himself, saying, 'What will I do, because I don't have room to store my crops?' He said, 'This is what I will do. I will pull down my barns, and build bigger ones, and there I will store all my grain and my goods. I will tell my soul, "Soul, you have many goods laid up for many years. Take your ease, eat, drink, be merry. But God said to him,* **you foolish one, tonight your soul is required of you. The things which you have prepared—whose will they be?'* *So is he who lays up treasure for himself, and is not rich toward God.***

God does not want us to worry about tomorrow. He does not want us to worry about what we will eat or drink, not even what we will wear. He has us covered just to do His will and build up our treasures in heaven according to Luke 12:22-34 *He said to His disciples, Therefore I tell you, do not be anxious for your life, what you will eat, nor yet for your body, what you will wear. Life is more than food, and the body is more than clothing. Consider the ravens: they do not sow, they do not reap, they have no warehouse or barn, and God feeds them. How much more valuable are you than birds! Which of you by being anxious can add a cubit to his height? If then you are not able to do even the least things, why are you anxious about the rest? Consider the lilies, how they grow. They do not toil, neither do they spin; yet I tell you, even Solomon in all his glory was not arrayed like one of these. But if this is how God clothes the grass in the field, which today exists, and tomorrow is cast into the oven, how much more will he clothe you, O you of little faith?* **Do not seek what you will eat or what you will drink; neither be anxious. For the nations of the world seek of these things, but your Father knows that you need these things. But seek God's Kingdom, and all these things will be added to you. Do not be afraid, little flock, for it is your Father's good pleasure to give you the Kingdom. Sell that which you have, and give gifts to the needy. Make for yourselves purses which do not grow old, a treasure in the heavens that does not fail, where no thief approaches, neither moth destroys. For where your treasure is, there will your heart be also.** WEB

God is the Source of our resources. We must learn how to tap into the Source of the resources. This acronym was stated in church a few times. I do not know the origin of the acronym: The Bible Is Basic Instructions Before Leaving Earth.

Despite what people may think and say about us. Even what we may have said about another. We may have even stopped speaking to each other for a while. Besides God we are all each other, when one struggle we all struggle.

When one is up, we are all up naturally and spiritually. We must pray for one another, When one rejoices, rejoice with them your turn will come too,

As a family individually we are fingers but when we close all those fingers, we make a strong fist and a powerful blow. We must sow encouraging words and actions to our family like love and forgiveness. Even if you are not around each other. Especially when you come together to give and receive love.

When you change others will praise you and not you YOURSELF. They will see your good works and glorify your Father which is in heaven.

Some will even talk bad about the new you but do not let them stop you or cause you to come out of your new character.

Satan comes, and tries to take away the word which has been sown in you. Let the Word of God take root in you. When oppression or persecution arises because of the Word do not stumble and if you do stumble and fall, get back up.

Do not allow the cares of this world, and the deceitfulness of riches, and the lusts of other things enter in and choke the word out of you and make you become unfruitful. Hear the word, receive it, and bear fruit. Hold your peace and let the Lord fight your battles. Give and it will be given to you. Sow and reap your harvest from the Lord

CHAPTER 44

BReaKiNG SOUL TieS

I am going to share this powerful Information with you on SOUL TIES (twine). When the two become one they are no more twine. When you pray, you must pray to God for a spiritual divorcement from every person you ever had intimacy with. CALL THEM OUT BY NAME. If you do not remember the names just call out the nature or place associated with the action? This must be done every time someone you slept with pops into your head, heart, or spirit. This will cause your spirits to untwine from that person that you have made that ungodly tie with. Even if it is with a person, you are with and you are not married to them. That is what you need to get yourselves together in the eyes of God. There are two options here: to get married or separate. Do not deceive yourselves once you have been in an intimate relation with a person it will, be hard to live together and abstain from sex. It does not matter if you were in a committed relationship or not, you cannot just say we are going to be around each other alone but we are going to abstain. Both parties are accountable to making it right in God's eyes. Gods' ways are not like our ways therefore we are not to seek the opinions of others. Many close friends and family will agree with you or try to stop you even if you are right or wrong. Whatever the Lord's will is for your lives if it is meant to be then no more soul ties you can truly be one. If it is not meant to be then there is freedom in Christ. Not free and single ready to mingle but free to dedicate your body to be used by the Lord until you are ready to do it God's way when two are willing to become one in marriage.

Reason both parties need to do this is because your spirit is still connected with the spirit of the person you are intimate with. Also, because your spirits are soul tied with everyone they slept and so one. Let us briefly look at the concept according to Scripture 1 Corinthians 6:13-16 *But the body is not for sexual immorality, but for the Lord; and the Lord for the body. Now God raised up the Lord, and will also raise us up by* *his power. Don't you know that your bodies are members of Christ? Shall I then take the members of Christ, and make them members of a prostitute? May it never be! Or do not you know that he who is **joined to a prostitute is one body? For, the two, says he, "will become one flesh.*** _{WEB}

Even the ones that raped, molested, fondled or any form of acts of violations you too must pray their spirit from you. Pray their spirit from you so you can be truly healed, set free & delivered. When some people act unseemly, they are unaware of the spirits passed down to them by these acts. Often behaviors that you have not seen before in you or the victim who has been affected by the list mentioned above. One may begin acting like the persons you have been involved with or someone they have been with. This is because you have knowingly or unknowingly become one with them WILLINGLY OR UNWILLINGLY. In the areas of any ungodly sexual acts. Proverb 18:22 *Whoever finds a wife finds a good thing, and obtains favor of Yahweh.* _{WEB}

Hebrews 13:4 *Let marriage be held in honor among all, and let the bed be undefiled: but God will judge the sexually immoral and adulterers.* _{WEB}

1 Corinthians 6:18 *Flee sexual immorality! "Every sin that a man does is outside the body," but he* or she *who commits sexual immorality sins against his* or her *own body.* _{WEB}

We must break the soul ties and destroy them at the root.
It starts with you and me in our own lives. AMEN

We once were ones who were not going to inherit the Kingdom of God but we were washed in the cleansing blood of Jesus in 1 Corinthians 6:11 Such *were some of you, but you were washed. But you were sanctified. But you were justified in the name of the Lord Jesus, and in the Spirit of our God.* _{WEB}

Romans 12:3 *For I say, through the grace that was given me, to every person who is among you, **not to think of himself** or **herself** more highly than he or she **ought to think**; but to think reasonably, as **God has apportioned to each person a measure of faith.*** _{WEB}

CHAPTER 45

HiNDeR

We must not be focused on judging one another and their sins. We must be mindful and prayerful not to put obstacles in the way of others that may obstruct or trip them. According to Romans 14:13 *Therefore let us not judge one another anymore, but rather determine this—**not to put an obstacle or an obstacle in a brother's** and sister's way.* _{WEB}

If we are indulging in sin the Lord will not hear us according to Psalm 66:18 **If I had cherished iniquity in my heart, the Lord would not have listened.** _{WEB}

We must check our own motives in our heart. James 4:3 **You ask and do not receive, because you ask wrongly, to spend it on your passions.** _{WEB}

This is a way that can hinder the prayer of an individual. It is mentioned that God does not hear a sinner's prayer.

All sinners must come into true repentance if they want God to hear their prayer. John 9:31 *We know that God does not listen to sinners, but if anyone is a worshipper of God, and does His will, He listens to Him.* _{WEB}

We all have sinned and come short of God's glory. If anyone says they have no sin they have the sin of being a liar. We must come into true repentance. This does not make us sinless but it makes us sin less.

A husband's prayers can be hindered. Look at the following Scripture to see why his prayer might be hindered. 1 Peter 3:7 *You husbands, in the same way, live with your wives according to knowledge, giving honor to the woman, as to the weaker vessel, as being also joint heirs of the grace of life; that your prayers may not be hindered.* _{WEB}

When we are assigned the work of the Lord we can be hindered. Romans 1:11-13 World English Bible *for I long to see you, **that I may impart to you some spiritual gift**, to the end that you may be established; that is, that I with you may be encouraged in you, each of us by the other's faith, both yours and mine. Now I do not desire to have you unaware, brothers, that **I often planned to come to you, and was hindered so far, that I might have some fruit among you also**, even as among the rest of the Gentiles.*

When we pray, we must forgive so that God can forgive us as found in Mark 11:25 in the World English Bible states *whenever you stand praying, forgive, if you have anything against anyone; so that your Father, who is in heaven, may also forgive you your transgressions.*

CHAPTER 46

SOME EAGLE NEED TO HEAR THIS

Isaiah 40:31 *But those who wait for Yahweh will renew their strength. They will mount up with wings like eagles. They will run, and not be weary. They will walk, and not faint.* _{WEB}

"To those who have hope in the LORD He will renew their strength. They will soar on wings like eagles; they will run and not grow weary; they will walk and not be faint". When an eagle flies, they soar, not always flapping their wings like other birds. When they have soared a while, they must rest. If they do not rest, they soar too high & their feathers will begin to freeze and the feathers will fall. That is how eagles end up in the valley.

Psalm 23:4 *Even though I walk through the valley of the shadow of death, I will fear no evil, for You are with me. Your rod and Your staff, they comfort me.* _{WEB}

If you are an eagle, you do not want to fall in the valley because you become prey to other birds and animals. You cannot just flap your wings and fly out of the valley like other birds. Eagles need a running start to fly. Other birds know how to flap their wings from a standpoint & take off.

When you reach your mountain top that is not the time to celebrate. When you reach the top of the mountain that is the time to pluck off those dead feathers to prepare for the next flight.

When you take your next flight and begin to soar. Know how to rest while you are soaring. Do not experience burn out, many leaders experience burn out. When you get on the mountain top that is your place of mounting up on wings as an eagle after you have taken the necessary steps. Remember it is not the time to run around celebrating. It is time to pluck off the dead feathers that have gotten frozen during the flights. It is time for your strength to be renewed. Renewed so that you can run and not be weary & walk and not faint.

When it is time for an eagle to fly, they take off running. They do not get weary or faint because they took the time to do what was necessary when they were on the mountain top. If they do not apply the necessary steps then they will not have enough strength for the journey. Then they will fall during flight or fall right off the mountain top. Now if you do fall, pray that it is in an Appalachian Mountain not the Rocky Mountain. Why? Because the Appalachian Mountain valleys are still higher than other mountain tops.

God makes provision in the valley. It is said that He is the Lily of the valley. Many lilies are white which represents purity. What is growing on the lilies under the ground are good for food.

Jesus is the Bright and Morning Star. He is the Son and the natural sun is shining to provide light and heat.

The rain waters the valley as it rolls down the mountains to provide water.

There are caves in the mountains and trees in the valley to provide shade and shelter.

There is so much to learn about the valley experience that's why Scripture says yes though I walk through the valley. When walking it requires putting one foot in front of the other foot. I heard even if you march in place, you will never put your foot in the same exact place again. When we are in the valley it is not the time to fear evil because God is with you. He promises to never leave us nor forsake us.

Yes, though you walk through the valley of the shadow of death. A shadow is a dark reflection of an image. The silhouette will cast depending on where the person is standing or walking in-between its rays and a surface area.

We are not to not fear any evil because the Lord is our Shepherd. If the Lord be our Shepherd, then death is nothing but a shadow. Fear is that false thing that takes shape as real. Especially when we believe the lies of the enemy.

We can know and say that God is with us, His rod and His staff comforts us. When you have hope in the Lord you will be able to get up. There are some eagles stuck in the valley because they have adapted to it. They have become friends with other birds, they have hooked up with some chickens. They have patty caked; sugar coated & watered down the Word of God. Many have gotten encouraged to stay longer than they should have stayed. You may have given up. DON'T GIVE UP!

Scripture tells us do not get weary in doing well we will reap a harvest if you faint not. You have crows pecking at you when you get up to a certain level. KEEP GOING! Just pluck off them dead feathers & get a running start, take off & soar. The next time you need to rest you know what it is for. It is to renew your strength & not to celebrate it. God got you to be the eagle He made you to be. Amen

CHAPTER 47

faiTH

Focus All In The Hope

Faith focuses all in the hope and God is our Hope. When we have faith in God the substances of the things we hope for can become manifested evidence. Those things that cannot be seen or not tangible can become. Hebrews 11:1 *Now faith is assurance of things hoped for, proof of things not seen.* WEB

First, we ought to know without faith we cannot please God. If we do not believe Him or believe He is real do not expect anything from Him. God loves us and gives us time. Hebrews 11:6 *Without faith it is impossible to be well pleasing to Him, for he who comes to God must believe that He exists, and that He is a rewarder of those who seek Him.* WEB

According to the World's English Bible found in Romans 3:3-4 *For what if some were without faith? Will their lack of faith nullify the faithfulness of God? May it never be! Yes, let God be found true, but every man is a liar.* In Romans 3:23 *all have sinned, and fall short of the glory of God.*

Scripture tells us on faith and works, one without the other both then your faith and your works are dead. James 2:18 *Yes, a man will say, "You have faith, and I have works." Show me your faith without works, and I by my works will show you, my faith.* WEB

Let us see what is said in James 2:14-17 *What good is it, my brothers, if a man says he has faith, but has no works? Can faith save him? And if a brother or sister is naked and in lack of daily food, and one of you tells them, "Go in peace. Be warmed and filled;" yet you didn't give them the things the body needs, what good is it? Even so faith, if it has no works, is dead in itself. James 2:19-26 You believe that God is one. You do well. The demons also believe, and shudder. But do you want to know, vain man, that faith apart from works is dead? Wasn't Abraham our father justified by works, in that he offered up Isaac his son on the altar? You see that faith worked with his works, and by works faith was perfected. So, the Scripture was fulfilled which says, "Abraham believed God, and it was accounted to him as righteousness," Genesis 15:6 and he was called the friend of God. You see then that by works, a man is justified, and not only by faith. In the same way, wasn't Rahab the prostitute also justified by works, in that she received the messengers and sent them out another way? For as the body apart from the spirit is dead, even so faith apart from works is dead.* _{WEB}

In 1 Thessalonians 2:13 *For this cause we also thank God without ceasing, that, when you received from us the word of the message of God, you accepted it not as the word of men, but, as it is in truth, the word of God, which also works in you who believe.* _{WEB}

Also in 1 Thessalonians 1:3 *remembering without ceasing your work of faith and labor of love and patience of hope in our Lord Jesus Christ, before our God and Father.* _{WEB}

When we pray, we must believe. It is said in the world to hope and pray for the best but prepare for the worst. However, that is contrary to the word of God. When we ask God, anything asks in faith. James 1:6-7 *But let Him ask in faith, without any doubting, for he who doubts is like a wave of the sea, driven by the wind and tossed. For let that man not think that he will receive anything from the Lord.* _{WEB}

In Luke 18:1-8 World English Bible Parable of the persistent widow woman: *He also spoke a parable to them that they must always pray, and not give up, saying, "There was a judge in a certain city who did not fear God, and didn't respect man. A widow was in that city, and she often came to him, saying, Defend me from my adversary! He would not for a while, but afterward he said to himself, Though I neither fear God, nor respect man, yet because this widow bothers me, I will defend her, or else she will wear me out by her continual coming. The Lord said, listen to what the unrighteous judge says. Won't God avenge His chosen ones, who are crying out to Him day and* *night, and yet He exercises patience with them? I tell you that He will avenge them quickly. Nevertheless, **when the Son of Man comes, will He find faith on the earth?*** _{WEB}

The enemy is trying to steal our faith in God. Do not allow him or anyone to rob you of your faith in God. We all have faith in something but our faith is to be in God. God has given everyone a portion of faith and we are not think more of ourselves than we ought to according to Romans 12:3 *For I say, through the grace that was given me, to every man who is among you, not to think of himself more highly than he ought to think; but to think reasonably, as God has apportioned to each person a measure of faith.* _{WEB}

Romans 1:17 *For in it is revealed God's righteousness from faith to faith. As it is written, "But the righteous shall live by faith."* _{WEB}

We ought to replace our unbelief with faith and nothing will be impossible for us in Matthew 17:20 World English Bible Jesus *said to them, Because of your unbelief. For most certainly I tell you, **if you have faith as a grain of mustard seed, you will tell this mountain, move from here to there, and it will move; and nothing will be impossible for you.***

Cite

Source: *https://bible.knowing-jesus.com/web*

Source: https://bible.knowing-jesus.com/phrases/Kingdom-of-Heaven/type/web

Source: https://bible.knowing-jesus.com/phrases/Kingdom-of-God /type/web

aBOUT THe aUTHOR

Sonya C. Greene-Pough is the author of a poetry book "Peculiar Lives Being Changed Through Poetry Giving God the Gory Lifting Up the Name of Jesus". She is a graduate of Jamison School of Ministry where she received her Bachelors in Theology. She was ordained as a Lay Pastor, later licensed, and ordained as a minister.

She is a graduate of ACT College where she received an Associate's Degree in Applied Health Science in Medical Assistant. Then she became a Nationally Registered Certified Medical Assistant and a Nationally Registered Certified Phlebotomy Technician. She is now married with four adult children and six living grandchildren. She is currently an author, school bus driver, and business owner. She talks about her Lord and Savior Jesus/Yashua everywhere she goes.

Printed in the United States
by Baker & Taylor Publisher Services